THE LIFE
OF POETRY

Publication of this book is made possible in part by grants from
the Eric Mathieu King Fund of The Academy of American
Poets and The Massachusetts Foundation for the Humanities.

BOOKS BY MURIEL RUKEYSER

PROSE

Houdini (Play)
The Traces of Thomas Hariot
The Orgy
The Colors of the Day (Play)
One Life
The Middle of the Air (Play)
Willard Gibbs

POETRY

The Collected Poems of Muriel Rukeyser
The Gates
Breaking Open
29 Poems
The Speed of Darkness
The Outer Banks
Waterlily Fire: Poems 1935–1962
Body of Waking
Selected Poems
Elegies
Orpheus
The Green Wave
Beast in View
The Soul and Body of John Brown
Wake Island
A Turning Wind
U.S. 1
Theory of Flight

THE LIFE
OF POETRY

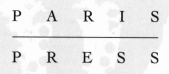

BY MURIEL RUKEYSER

WITH A NEW FOREWORD
BY JANE COOPER

PARIS

PRESS

ASHFIELD, MASSACHUSETTS
1996

This book, or parts thereof, may not be reproduced in any
form, except for the purposes of review, without the express
permission of the publisher. For information address
Paris Press, Inc., P.O. Box 487, Ashfield, MA 01330.
Since this page cannot accommodate all the copyright
notices, the acknowledgments on page 215
constitute an extension of this copyright page.

*Paris Press gratefully acknowledges the generous assistance
of those individuals and organizations who support our work.*

Cover design by Ewa Nogiec
Photograph on back cover by William L. Rukeyser
Index by Patricia Hollander Gross

Library of Congress Cataloging-in-Publication Data

Rukeyser, Muriel, 1913-1980
The life of poetry / by Muriel Rukeyser ; with a new introduction
by Jane Cooper.
p.   cm.
Includes bibliographical references and index.
ISBN 0-9638183-3-3 (alk. paper)
1. Poetry.   I. Title.
PN1031.R75   1996
811.009—dc20   96-22476
                                                   CIP

1st ed. New York: Current Books, © 1949 Muriel Rukeyser
Reprinted New York: William Morrow & Co., © 1974 Muriel Rukeyser
First Paris Press Edition, 1996

3 4 5 6 7 8 9 0

Printed in the United States of America

CONTENTS

NOTE FROM
THE PUBLISHER

It is with great pride that Paris Press publishes Muriel Rukeyser's *The Life of Poetry*. This book ranks among the most essential works of twentieth century literature; it is saving, challenging. In *The Life of Poetry* Rukeyser examines the ways in which poetry can revive democracy and improve the quality of life for the people of the United States, and for poets, artists, and creative individuals everywhere.

This publication of *The Life of Poetry* is a revised edition of the earlier texts, originally published by Current Books, 1949, and reprinted by William Morrow & Co., 1974. For the first time, the chapter subheadings listed in the table of contents are carried over into the body of the book. An index and a new foreword by the poet Jane Cooper are included. Also for the first time, a few factual errors and some misquotations and misattributions of poems and other works mentioned are corrected. Some punctuation is corrected as well, always respecting Rukeyser's usual admonition, "Please believe the punctuation!"

The Life of Poetry is not a book of criticism nor is it a literary treatise. It is a book that breaks boundaries and assumptions about the place of literature and the arts in American life. Rukeyser suggests that by living with the senses and the imagination open, living with poetry, human beings can prosper and attain peace. Remarkably, Rukeyser's words are as necessary and provocative now as when the book was first published, in 1949.

JAN FREEMAN

NOTE FROM
THE AUTHOR

A way to allow people to feel the meeting of their consciousness and the world, to feel the full value of the meanings
of emotions and ideas in their relations with each other, and to
understand, in the glimpse of a moment, the freshness of things
and their possibilities.... There is an art which gives us that
way; and it is, in our society, an outcast art.

In this book, I have tried to track down the resistances to
poetry, with every kind of "boredom" and "impatience," the
name-calling which says that poetry is "intellectual and obscure
and confused and sexually suspect." How much of this is true,
and how much can be traced to the corruption of consciousness?
We can see what these attitudes mean, in impoverishment of the
imagination, to audience and to artist, both of whom of course
are deeply affected.

I have tried to go behind the resistance, which is often a fear
of poetry, and to show what might be ahead of this culture in
conflict, with its background of strength and antagonism. If we
are free, we are free to choose a tradition, and we find in the past
as well as the present our poets of outrage—like Melville—and
our poets of possibility—like Whitman.

Now the book goes on to the accepted arts, which meet
much less resistance in our culture, the arts in which we find

"applied poetry." The movies, jazz and the blues, writing with pictures, the Broadway theater and musical revues, and radio, are in a brilliant state of vitality and attractiveness. They share, however, the lack of language, and the emptiness of language in all of them indicates the same things: a hesitation before meanings, and a deep readiness and hunger for poetry, which is in the amusement arts unconsciously, as it is to a greater extent in the people.

The relations of poetry are, for our period, very close to the relations of science. It is not a matter of using the results of science, but of seeing that there is a meeting-place between all the kinds of imagination. Poetry can provide that meeting-place.

I have attempted to suggest a dynamics of poetry, showing that a poem is not its words or its images, any more than a symphony is its notes or a river its drops of water. Poetry depends on the moving relations within itself. It is an art that lives in time, expressing and evoking the moving relation between the individual consciousness and the world. The work that a poem does is a transfer of human energy, and I think human energy may be defined as consciousness, the capacity to make change in existing conditions. It appears to me that to accept poetry in these meanings would make it possible for people to use it as an "exercise," an enjoyment of the possibility of dealing with the meanings in the world and in their lives.

M.R.

ACKNOWLEDGMENTS

I should like to acknowledge the contribution of the following to this book: F. O. Matthiessen, Marie de L. Welch, Hallie Flanagan, and Freda Koblick, for whose reactions to this material I have been especially grateful; the people of the poetry workshops I have offered; Isobel Cerney, Alexandra Docili and Peter Docili, and Antoinette Willson, who at several stages helped with the typing of the manuscript; and my son Laurie, whose waking and whose sleep each played its part.

Most of the material of this book was first presented in the form of talks on poetry and communication, at Vassar College in 1940, at the California Labor School in 1945 and 1948, and at Columbia University in 1946; and in other lectures and broadcasts.

I wish here to thank Henry Noble MacCracken, David Jenkins, Holland Roberts, and Russell Potter, for their invitations and their backing of the lectures.

Selections from this book have appeared in the following: *Twice a Year*, *Berkeley*, and *Poets of the Mid-Century*.

[For reasons of space, additional acknowledgments are continued on page 215.]

FOREWORD:
MEETING-PLACES

Imagine Muriel Rukeyser in 1949, as *The Life of Poetry* is about to be published. Imagine you are her reader, not only today but then. She is thirty-five, and this is her seventh full-length book. Already there have been five significant collections of poems, the pioneering, unauthorized biography of a world-class American scientist, Willard Gibbs, and now this statement of belief. How will you receive it? Can you accept poetry as an "exercise" on which your life may depend? Surely by now she has earned your trust. Through invention and action, she has earned the authority to speak.

Action? The poems in a real sense have been actions. The biography, in its assumption of the unity of all modes of creative imagination, is an action. How much does it matter that she has also, repeatedly, put her body on the line?

At nineteen she was arrested in Alabama at the trial of the "Scottsboro Boys," nine black youths falsely accused of raping two white women. At twenty-two she was at Gauley Bridge, West Virginia, making a unique poem/documentary about tunnel-drillers dying of silicosis—a clear case of industrial greed. In the same year, 1936, she saw the first days of the Spanish Civil War from the anarchist stronghold of Barcelona and was told to return home to bear witness. By 1949, unmarried, she is the working mother of a two-year-old son, whose father has turned his back on them both.

Nineteen forty-nine: a year poised between the affirmations of international responsibility that followed World War II and the wave of fear, suspicion, and repressiveness that found its embodiment in Senator Joe McCarthy. In poetry, it is the heyday of the New (she calls them the "old") Critics.

She is a large, handsome, dark-maned woman, with her head tossed back, gaze very direct from under soaring eyebrows, shoulders squared, but with unexpectedly delicate hands, ankles, and feet. You will not fail to notice her, entering a room. Perhaps you have already been listening for a voice not loud but resonant, rising musically from the very pit of the body. Probably she has always been subtle, and quick to feel hurt. Yet she is witty, both jovial and sly. A begetter of storms. An unpredictable force. Now imagine she is coming to meet you.... A broadly smiling friend.

Disarmingly, at the beginning of Chapter XII of *The Life of Poetry,* Muriel Rukeyser will herself address you: "My one reader, you reading this book, who are you? what is your face like, your hand holding the pages, the child forsaken in you, who now looks through your eyes at mine?" [1]

In the same way I, the maker of introductions—back now in our mutual present—would like to address you, the reader of this new edition, asking what, almost fifty years after the book was originally published, you might want to know. It is a book passionate and timely. An essential resource that for too long has been denied us, out of print. Still, there are ways I might help to locate you, matters of fact and relationship I can hope to point out.

And there are other ways in which only you can do your own work.

Let us start with the idea of war, and what it means, what it meant to Muriel Rukeyser, to be an American. And why, in an argument for poetry as "the type of creation in which we may live and which will save us," [2] must we begin with fear and the resistances to poetry? And what did she understand by "form"?

> *I lived in the first century of world wars.*
> *Most mornings I would be more or less insane....*
> —"Poem"[3]

In a statement written for Oscar Williams's 1945 anthology *The War Poets*, Muriel Rukeyser said, "For myself, war has been in my writing since I began. The first public day that I remember was the False Armistice of 1918." Then she went on to explain—as she will explain in *The Life of Poetry*—that in her view, the task of poets during World War II was fully to confront the meanings of the war against fascism, and by so doing to help bring peoples together, to be part of the movement toward peace and the "living, changing goal."[4] Poetry, because it demands full consciousness on the part of the writer, and full response on the part of the witness/reader to the truths of feeling, because there is this genuine exchange, could have been the type of such a movement. But the moment was lost, the meanings were lost in our will to win; poetry gave way to advertising.

The Life of Poetry is based on lectures given at Vassar College in 1940, just after the outbreak of World War II in Europe, and at the California Labor School and Columbia University in 1945, 1946, and 1948, soon after its end. So World War II can be seen as the matrix for its arguments, lending them an almost desperate force. Yet, significantly, the book's opening scene recalls an earlier, doomed struggle against fascism, the Spanish Civil War, which had been Rukeyser's own "moment of proof." It seems she was only in Barcelona for the first five days of the conflict, in the course of which she fell in love with a German athlete, Otto Boch, who had come to take part in the Anti-Fascist Olympics and afterwards lost his life in the fight against

Franco. But this love, and "the long defeat that brings us what we know," [5] as she would still call it almost forty years later, became part of her inclusive myth, shaping from within her subsequent commitments and her writing.

The opening scene is lyrical, almost hallucinatory in its intimacy. She is on the deck of a small ship at night, a ship carrying away from Spain all the foreigners who could not be of immediate use to the Republic. Darkness, small, trembling lights along the seacoast, hesitant voices of the passengers, a few stars.... At first it seems the quiet of the conversations that is most striking. Or a sort of rhyme, that will be familiar to anyone who has watched the onset of hostilities: "In time of crisis, we summon up our strength," soon changing to "In time of crises of the spirit, we are aware of all our need." A man's voice, a refugee's voice, interrupts: "And poetry—among all this—where is there a place for poetry?" Did he actually exist, that man? Does it matter? She is able to answer: "Then I began to say what I believe."[6]

It is the condition of war, which now seems a more or less permanent, everyday condition across half the world, like a low-grade infection that can flare into epidemic, that makes us realize how we hunger and thirst after poetry. And how we discount it. This is the ground of the present book.

All her life Muriel Rukeyser would be alert to the terrors of war, impending wars, repressive regimes. One wants to read *The Life of Poetry* for the light it sheds on work she did after 1949 as well as what was done before. Her last three celebrated books of poems, written when she was under increasing threat from diabetes and a series of strokes, were among other things a record of her resistance to American involvement in Vietnam, including a trip she took to Hanoi during the bombing, and of her journey to South Korea, as President of PEN American Center, to protest in person the solitary confinement of poet Kim Chi

Ha. Again, she would put her body and her writing on the line. (The Korean experience is central to "The Gates," the last poem in her *Collected Poems*.) At the same time, she saw herself less as one who protests than as one who makes: "Wherever/ we protest/ we will go planting// Wherever/ I walk/ I will make."[7] Always the point of any struggle would be to help create peace, to bring peoples together. Or, as she said in a *New York Quarterly* craft interview in 1972: "It isn't that one brings life together—it's that one will not allow it to be torn apart."[8]

But even more important than her political presence during the final years was her understanding of the ways war enters deeply into our personal, daily lives, into our consciousness, and then more deeply still, into the subconscious impulses and motions of the spirit. The last three books especially are memorable for their recognition that whatever we despise, we are; that every morning, in order to begin to be non-violent, we must acknowledge our own violence. And then there is her continued recognition that this country was founded in division. The cornerstone of a church on New Haven's green is a monument to regicide. The framers of the Constitution made sure of a system of checks and balances; as she notes in this book, having killed the native peoples and broken the land to the plow, our fathers embraced the ideals of the Enlightenment, hoping for a government of reconciliation. Yet even as I write, our nominally two-party Congress seems to be tearing itself apart or lapsing into paralysis. And what can be said for the financial wizards who, in the face of deficit and unemployment, only strengthen our dependence on the arms race?

In 1949 Rukeyser wrote: "American poetry has been part of a culture in conflict."

And: "We are a people tending toward democracy at the level of hope; on another level, the economy of the nation, the empire of business within the republic, both include in their basic premise the concept of perpetual warfare. It is the history of the idea of war that is beneath our other histories." [9]

> And the child sitting alone planning her hope:
> I want to write for my race.   But what race will you speak,
> being American?   I want to write for the living.
> —"Fourth Elegy. The Refugees"[10]

She used to say, "I want to catch for my country." Did she still, somewhere at the heart of the joke, imagine herself as Joan of Arc in the guise of Yogi Berra?

Perhaps there is nothing that so separates us from Muriel Rukeyser, at our sour end of the century, as her capacity for faith. We can accept the ground bass of war and the consciousness of war more easily than her passionate vision of what it could mean to be an American. Ultimately, it would mean reaching out, relationship, the dissolving of boundaries, speaking, touching, one world. But she came of age during the thirties. And not only does she invoke, through her opening scene of leaving Spain, the Popular Front in the war against fascism abroad, but her work asks to be set in context with Hart Crane's "The Bridge," John Dos Passos's trilogy *U.S.A.*, James Agee's *Let Us Now Praise Famous Men*, with criticism by Van Wyck Brooks and F. O. Matthiessen, photographs and documentaries by the great black-and-white photographers of the Depression years. It was a period of the most intense interest in all things American, and American populist novels, at least (for instance, *The Grapes of Wrath*), were widely read and praised. Rukeyser's first major long poem, "Theory of Flight" (1935), ends "Say yes, people./ Say yes./ YES,"[11] which can make us smile. Her second book (1938) is called *U.S.1.*

American historians and some critics were engaged in radical reassessments of the American legacy and of the giants of our nineteenth-century literature: Emerson, Hawthorne, Poe, Whitman, Dickinson, Thoreau, Melville. Muriel Rukeyser, in *The Life of Poetry* and elsewhere, is engaged in recovering her own usable past, so that she, and we, can move forward with fuller consciousness into the future. "If we are free," she says—meaning, if we are a free citizenry—"we are free to choose a tradition." [12]

Elsewhere her heroes are Willard Gibbs, the mathematical physicist, Albert Pinkham Ryder, painter of the sea, John Jay Chapman, man of letters, Ann Burlak, labor organizer, Charles Ives, composer on American themes; and John Brown and Wendell Willkie, political visionaries who seemed, at their historical moments, to fail; Houdini and Lord Timothy Dexter, anomalies in any pantheon. How many of their stories are familiar to us, even now? Of all these she made biographies, in verse or prose or mixed media—the series of "Lives" that would occupy her to the end. All were Americans. Of the first five she pointed out, in 1939, that they were also New Englanders, "whose value to our generation is very great and only partly acknowledged." [13] She never wanted to write extensively about anyone who had already received his or her due, and it's worth noting how rarely any of her subjects is literary. For years she worked on a book, now lost, on Franz Boas, anthropologist who studied North American indigenous tribes. Only much later would she turn to several non-Americans, the last being Thomas Hariot, Elizabethan navigator, mathematician, naturalist, astronomer, who published the first *Brief and True Report* of Raleigh's Virginia, the "Indians" who lived there, and our native plants and animals.

No one has been more concerned to understand the nature of the American imagination. What is our peculiar genius as a people? That, I take it, would always be her question. And why, when a significant figure in any field has existed among us, is that person so often cut off, the work unremarked by creative thinkers in other fields, partially obscured or altogether lost?

Part Two and especially Part Three of *The Life of Poetry* comprise a brilliant exposition of the artistic experiences available to any attentive citizen in 1949. And here we can see how of her age yet ahead of her age—and ours, too—she was. She speaks movingly of the importance of Native American chants to our poetry, of jazz and the blues of Leadbelly and Bessie Smith, of a moment when Gene Kelly dances way beyond the confines of the film in which he stars. She loved our popular arts and saw how slick they could become, how American movies in particular (she had worked as a film editor and cutter) have a kind of athletic dazzle that enchants and distracts us but cannot satisfy our needs. How much is out there, she seems to be saying. How far we fall short.

For Muriel Rukeyser, whose file received from the Department of Justice only months before her death revealed she had been under F.B.I. surveillance for over forty years, was a patriot. You cannot understand the grief, the wild anger, nor the consistent, positive joy of this book unless you accept that.

> *The fear of poetry is the*
> *fear....*
> —"Reading Time: 1 Minute, 26 Seconds" [14]

Perhaps it is oddly a little reassuring to us that a book so positive in its essence begins with a litany of obstacles. Why is poetry feared? Because it demands full consciousness; it asks us to feel and it asks us to respond. Through poetry we are brought face to face with our world and we plunge deeply into ourselves, to a place where we sense "the full value of the meanings of emotions and ideas in their relations with each other, and...understand, in the glimpse of a moment, the freshness of things and their possibilities."[15] Through it, if we really give ourselves to the experience, we must be changed.

We resist change. Of poetry we say it's obscure, it's boring, what sex is he or she anyway, the one who wrote it? how could *I* share experience with her, with him? Who has the time? the energy? We expected more. We really wanted less. We are lazy, masked.

In the 1972 craft interview, Muriel Rukeyser agreed that matters did seem to have improved since 1949; her eleven-year-old nephew told her that most of the kids in his class were poets. She herself, along with many others, was going into classrooms to "read poems with" children and older people and to encourage them to write. One of her favorite assignments was to ask everyone to complete the sentence "I could not tell...." For in what we cannot say to anyone, in our most secret conflicts, lie curled, she believed, our inescapable poems.

In fact the situation had, and has, only superficially altered. If poetry is no longer exactly an "outcast" art in the United States, how profoundly is it accepted? How many citizens, at least after their very early twenties, are simply indifferent? They resist change. They close the book. They cannot remember, if they ever knew, when or if poetry was "useful."

But let's look at the dynamic here—that is, the dynamic of Rukeyser's own thought.

She always said that the pattern of her life was "first a no, then a yes." For instance when she sent the manuscript of her first book to Stephen Vincent Benét, judge of the Yale Younger Poets award and author of *John Brown's Body*, he initially turned it down, then wrote the next year asking to see it again and agreed to publish it. Similarly, she used to speak of the wave motion of an exemplary life. In the lives she chose to chronicle, she looked specifically for "the ways of getting past impossibility by changing phase."[16] The language came from Gibbs, the idea of transformation from Gibbs and also from Jung.

She said, "The reason I think that I came to do Gibbs was that I needed a language of transformation. I needed a language of a changing phase for the poem. And I needed a language that was not static, that did not see life as a series of points, but more as a language of water, and the things are in all these lives that I try to see in poems. Moving past one phase of one's own life—transformation, and moving past impossibilities. Things seen as impossibilities at the moment.... That meaning is a religious meaning. And a very common plain one too."[17]

She also pointed out how in "The Poem as Mask: *Orpheus*," as soon as she declares "No more masks! No more mythologies!"[18] "then the myth begins again. At that moment...the god lifts his hand."[19]

Does this suggest not only a way of looking at the great figures of the past whose stories still have meaning for us, and a way for the poem to grow organically from within, but also one reason why this book opens with the resistances to poetry?

What is important to understand is that the impossibilities are not negative. They too are part of the experience. Because of them, we go deeper.

At the beginning of Part Two of *The Life of Poetry*, Muriel Rukeyser discusses how in our culture "every quality is set *against*... another quality," and how good and evil are always taken as opposites, not as two problems in their "interplay."[20] Again, "It is the history of the idea of war that is beneath our other histories.... But around and under and above it is another reality... the history of possibility."[21] Can we accept both these statements without automatically trying to fit them into a binary system? And what about "Outrage and possibility are in all the poems we know"? [22]

For her the two great exemplars from nineteenth-century American literature are Melville, the poet of outrage, and Whitman, the poet of possibility. Melville, she says, wrote again and again in his prose of the problem of evil, and he was the first among us to do so, "but in the poems, the oppositions turn to music." [23] Nobody saw more clearly and piercingly the effects of sexual mismatch; his is one of the great, disabused voices of the Civil War or any war.

For Whitman, on the other hand, the quest was for integration, first of the self and his sexuality, then of his experiences as a wartime nurse. In accepting himself, he came to accept these United States. Without passivity, he learned to put the war behind him. "Whitman's fight for reconciliation was of profound value as a symbol," concludes Rukeyser. "The fight was the essential process of democracy: to remake and acknowledge the relationships, to find the truth and power in diversity...." [24]

> *Do I move toward form, do I use all my fears?*
> —"Double Ode" [25]

"Double Ode" is one of Muriel Rukeyser's very late poems. It is a complicated poem, addressed to her son and his wife, looking ahead to the birth of their first child and back to her own parents, and finally taking responsibility for the present moment in which the poet finds herself among "all the old gifts and wars." [26] In other words (no pun intended), it is a complicated "system of relations." I don't mean to discuss this or any poem in detail, but I would like to point out the series of one-syllable, simple words that anchor the closing line above:

DO   MOVE   FORM   USE   FEARS

"Do" and "move" need no gloss. They echo all through Rukeyser's work, from "Theory of Flight" on, small, active verbs summoning us to action. But there is a sequence of *oo*-sounds here that carries us forward to "use," a word of crucial importance in *The Life of Poetry*. How is it that we are never taught to *use* poetry? Poetry can be *useful* in providing us with a theater of total human response. The remaining three words—"form," "use," "fears," the first and third of which are again linked by sound—are all in fact crucial to *The Life of Poetry*. What would it mean to learn to *use* our *fears*? Must we redefine *fear* for the purposes of this book? Suppose *fears* are after all the "guardians" (a word that reverberates throughout the poem)? Have we considered how afraid we are of any real communication with another human being, of religious exploration, of risk-taking in politics, pure science, art? As Rilke's archaic torso of Apollo tells him he must change his life, so "the fear of poetry" is an index of its seriousness.

These five words are among the most ordinary. Yet we enter into them deeply, even freshly, because of their relations, and because of the weight and process of the whole poem leading up to them.

"Do I move toward form...?"

Nothing is more revolutionary in this frequently revolutionary book than the first two chapters of Part Four, in which Rukeyser derives her theory of form from science—not the materials of science but its method. From Gibbs she took the idea that the whole is actually simpler than its parts, and also, that "our time depends, not on single points of knowledge, but on clusters and combinations." [27] Her imagination fired by analogy, she found in science a "system of relations" that could be expressed symbolically. [28] Especially important is Gibbs's "Phase Rule."

What are the implications of this for poetry? "I needed a language of a changing phase for the poem...a language that was not static, that did not see life as a series of points, but more as a language of water."[29]

Earlier she has spoken of Whitman's rhythms, which set his breathing and heartbeat "against an ideal of water at the shore, not beginning nor ending, but endlessly drawing in, making forever its forms of massing and falling among the breakers, seething in the white recessions of its surf, never finishing, always making a meeting-place."[30]

Many people, she remarks, "think of form in poetry as a framework."[31] Or they focus on the poem's images, which are its most dramatic element, or its musical structure, or a few extraordinary words. The New Critics seemed to want to reduce the poem to crystalline moments, ignoring the life of the poet and the world but most of all the poem's own mysterious, contagious, self-renewing energy.

Instead Rukeyser proposes—following D'Arcy Thompson now as well as Gibbs—that the great poems are always organic, as forms in nature are organic. They grow by "clusters and combinations," through time; they find their true direction as they proceed; and they never stand still but "fly through, and over"[32] any attempt to pin them down by analysis. They include material from the unconscious and welcome the unknown. More, "the work that a poem does is a transfer of human energy," from the poet through the poem to the fully responsible and responsive witness/reader. And now she takes a gigantic leap, tying the poet forever to the society and historical moment she or he shares with others: "I think human energy may be defined as consciousness, the capacity to make change in existing conditions."[33]

Characteristically (for the poem *is* an action), she goes on to describe the making of a specific poem, the first "Orpheus," and the making of one poet, herself. She explores the "confession to oneself made available to all," a type of which is the poem, and its powers to help us toward completeness. Honest and complicated to the end, though full of dreaming, she acknowledges that to make a poem is to release aggression, but since the release is appropriate, "it is creation."[34] As a poem moves in its dance of multiplicity, so she asks for a "society in motion, with many overlapping groups...above all, a society in which peace is not lack of war, but a drive toward unity."[35]

"We are a people tending toward democracy at the level of hope." At the level of hope, then, but characteristically, the last word in *The Life of Poetry* is "peace."

Reader, rarely will you encounter a mind or imagination of greater scope.

She liked to say that poems are meeting-places, and certainly as one composes a poem there is a sense of seeing farther than usual into the connections of things, and then of bringing intense pressure to bear on those connections, until they rise into full consciousness for oneself and others. The farther out along the frontiers of awareness the original elements of the poem lie, or the more deeply they are hidden, the more strenuous the poet's task and the more essential the poem. Its order and music must be such as to create a new whole.

Something of the same process of searching out and combining has obviously gone into *The Life of Poetry*. You may not find this an easy book. But it has the rigor and exitement of a fine poem: reach, density, relatedness. It will require your concentration, as it required hers.

Lately we have heard a lot about the importance, psychologically speaking, of boundaries. It seems that our health depends on clear boundaries between the self and others. But Muriel

Rukeyser didn't believe in boundaries. She wanted a poetry of becoming, of recognitions, poems like a constellation or the sea. Her arguments soar and fall back; they are never finished but recur and overlap. And at the very heart of this book is an ideal of boundaries dissolved. She felt that the unity of science, the unity of the poem, the promise of air and space travel and ecology in its broadest terms, the threat and promise of nuclear energy, and the hunger of peoples everywhere for international communication, would all help to convince us that we live in one world. Politics might seem to subvert this vision, but in our own time the electronic media confirm it every day.

For she was a visionary. One of the great, necessary poets of our country and century, whose value to the present generation is only beginning to be acknowledged, like Whitman she was a poet of possibility. I have tried to suggest here how she would never separate poetry from history or her active life in the world, would never separate (though this is a longer stretch for most of us) poetry from science. She believed in the identity of all modes of creative imagination, and she saw in the stories of certain men and women, in no way supernatural, the same mythical patterns that inform our indispensable poems.

Furthermore, she was a "she-poet." As she told her interviewer in 1972, "Anything I bring to this is because I am a woman. And this is the thing that was left out of the Elizabethan world, the element that did not exist. Maybe, maybe, maybe that is what one can bring to life."[36]

I was lucky enough to be a friend of Muriel Rukeyser's for over twenty-five years. And while I didn't yet know her in 1949—I first met her only three or four years later—I have vivid recollections of how she looked and walked and laughed and talked when she was, as they say, in her prime, and also of how she could storm and fall silent and then, slyly, start to joke again, or gaze at one generously and without defenses.

She died in 1980, of accumulated illnesses, at the age of sixty-six—not old, but consider how she had used herself! Since then—and here she becomes like one of her own characters, whose lives are oddly obscured—the *Collected Poems* and virtually all her single volumes have slipped out of print. An exception is *Willard Gibbs*, reissued by Ox Bow Press in 1988. Now, fortunately, a grand process of reclamation is under way. Recently, *A Muriel Rukeyser Reader*, poems and prose edited by Jan Heller Levi, with an introduction by Adrienne Rich, and *Out of Silence*, poems edited by Kate Daniels, have made a rich selection of her work newly available. It is to be hoped that a reprint of the *Collected Poems* will follow soon. Meanwhile her "Irish book," *The Orgy*, part myth, part memoir, is promised from Paris Press, and you hold this essential guide, *The Life of Poetry*, in your hand.

The same ideas are in all she wrote and taught.

Reader, she will want to change your life. No, she wants you to change it.

JANE COOPER

BIBLIOGRAPHY

Draves, Cornelia, and Fortunato, Mary Jane. "Craft Interview With Muriel Rukeyser." *The New York Quarterly* (1972), pp. 15–39. Later reprinted in *The Craft of Poetry,* edited by William Packard. Garden City, NY: Doubleday, 1974.

Rukeyser, Muriel. *The Collected Poems.* New York: McGraw-Hill Book Company, 1978.

———. *The Life of Poetry.* Ashfield, MA: Paris Press, 1996. Revised edition. New York: William Morrow & Company, Inc., 1974. Reprinted without textual changes from the original edition. New York: Current Books, 1949.

———. *A Turning Wind.* New York: Viking, 1939.

———. "War and Poetry." In *The War Poets,* edited by Oscar Williams, pp. 25–26. New York: John Day, 1945, quoted in Louise Kertesz. *The Poetic Vision of Muriel Rukeyser.* Baton Rouge and London: Louisiana State University Press, 1980.

———. *Willard Gibbs.* Garden City, NY: Doubleday, Doran, 1942.

FOOTNOTES

After the first mention, *The Collected Poems* is referred to as *CP* and *The Life of Poetry* as *LP*.

1. Muriel Rukeyser, *The Life of Poetry* (Ashfield, MA: Paris Press, 1996), p. 189.
2. *LP*, p. 213.
3. "Poem," Muriel Rukeyser, *The Collected Poems* (New York: McGraw-Hill Book Company, 1978), p. 450.
4. "War and Poetry," in *The War Poets*, edited by Oscar Williams, pp. 25–26, quoted in Louise Kertesz, *The Poetic Vision of Muriel Rukeyser* (Baton Rouge and London: Louisiana State University Press, 1980), p. 175.
5. "Neruda, the Wine," *CP*, p. 554.
6. *LP*, p.3.
7. "Wherever," *CP*, p. 514.
8. Cornelia Draves and Mary Jane Fortunato, "Craft Interview With Muriel Rukeyser," *The New York Quarterly*, (1972), p. 34.
9. *LP*, p. 61.
10. "Fourth Elegy. The Refugees," *CP*, p. 154.
11. "Theory of Flight," *CP*, p. 46.
12. *LP*, p. x.
13. Muriel Rukeyser, *A Turning Wind* (New York: Viking, 1939), unpaged.
14. "Reading Time: 1 Minute, 26 Seconds," *CP*, p. 161.
15. *LP*, p. x.
16. "Craft Interview," p. 32.
17. "Craft Interview," pp. 32–33.
18. "The Poem as Mask: Orpheus," *CP*, p. 435.
19. "Craft Interviw," p. 30.
20. *LP*, p. 64.
21. Ibid. p. 61.
22. Ibid. p. 66.
23. Ibid. p. 67.
24. Ibid. p. 78.
25. "Double Ode," *CP*, p. 543.
26. Ibid. p. 542.
27. Muriel Rukeyser, *Willard Gibbs* (Garden City, NY: Doubleday, Doran, 1942), p. 3.
28. *LP*, p. 165.
29. "Craft Interview," p. 32.
30. *LP*, p. 78.
31. Ibid. p. 30.
32. Ibid. p. 171.
33. Ibid. p. xi.
34. Ibid. pp. 212-213.
35. Ibid. p. 211.
36. "Craft Interview," p. 39.

To Henriette Durham

THE LIFE
OF POETRY

INTRODUCTION

In time of crisis, we summon up our strength.

Then, if we are lucky, we are able to call every resource, every forgotten image that can leap to our quickening, every memory that can make us know our power. And this luck is more than it seems to be: it depends on the long preparation of the self to be used.

In time of the crises of the spirit, we are aware of all our need, our need for each other and our need for our selves. We call up, with all the strength of summoning we have, our fullness. And then we turn; for it is a turning that we have prepared; and act. The time of the turning may be very long. It may hardly exist.

I think now of a boat on which I sailed away from the beginning of a war. It was nighttime, and over the deep fertile sea of night the voices of people talking quietly; some lights of the seacoast, faraway; some stars.

This was the first moment of stillness in days of fighting. We had seen the primitive beginnings of the open warfare of this period: men running through the silvery groves, the sniper whose gun would speak, as the bullet broke the wall beside you; a child staring upward at a single plane. More would come; in the city, the cars burned and blood streamed over the walls of houses and the horses shrieked; armies formed and marched out; the gypsies, the priests, in their purity and violence fought. Word from abroad was coming in as they asked us to meet in the summer leafy Square, and told us what they knew. They had seen how, as foreigners, we were deprived; how we were kept from, and wanted, above all things one: our responsibility.

This was a stroke of insight: it was true. "Now you have your responsibility," the voice said, deep, prophetic, direct, "go home: tell your peoples what you have seen."

We had seen a beginning. Much more would come.

I remember how the boys climbed into those trucks, with their ill-matched rifles, as the radio played Beethoven and Bing Crosby and the dances of the country. The machine guns clattered like a loud enormous palm tree, and a baby cried to its mother to come. On the floor of the train were strewn the foreign papers with their pictures printed dark: the possessed man, Nijinsky, giving his first interview from the sanatorium in all those years— the pictures of him, standing as he stood against the great black cross he years before had unrolled on the floor, dancing the insane dance, War and Death.

No darker than this night.

Yes, darker. For the night was living, all of us alive, the living breeze a flaw of coolness over the distant warmth of vineyards, over this central sea. The refugees on the boat were talking. There were people from many countries, thrown abruptly together in time of crisis, and speaking, somehow, the opinions which, later, their countries held.

I did not know this then. But we spoke as if we were shadows on that deck, shadows cast backward by some future fire of explosion.

We were on a small ship, five times past our capacity in refugees, sailing for the first port at peace. On the deck that night, people talked quietly about what they had just seen and what it might mean to the world. The acute scenes were still on our eyes, immediate and clear in their passion; and there were moments, too, in which we were outsiders and could draw away, as if we were in a plane and rose far, to a high focus above that coast, those cities and this sea, with sight and feelings sharper than before. Everything we had heard, some of all we loved and feared, had begun to be acted out. Our realization was fresh and young, we had seen the parts of our lives in a new arrangement. There were long pauses between those broken images of life, spoken in language after language.

Suddenly, throwing his question into talk not at all leading up to it—not seeming to—a man—a printer, several times a refugee —asked, "And poetry—among all this—where is there a place for poetry?"

Then I began to say what I believe.

PART ONE

THE
RESISTANCES

CHAPTER ONE

THE FEAR OF POETRY

In this moment when we face horizons and conflicts wider than ever before, we want our resources, the ways of strength. We look again to the human wish, its faiths, the means by which the imagination leads us to surpass ourselves.

If there is a feeling that something has been lost, it may be because much has not yet been used, much is still to be found and begun.

Everywhere we are told that our human resources are all *to be used*, that our civilization itself means the uses of everything it has—the inventions, the histories, every scrap of fact. But there is one *kind* of knowledge—infinitely precious, time-resistant more than monuments, here to be passed between the generations in any way it may be: never to be used. And that is poetry.

It seems to me that we cut ourselves off, that we impoverish ourselves, just here. I think that we are ruling out one source of power, one that is precisely what we need. Now, when it is hard to hold for a moment the giant clusters of event and meaning that every day appear, it is time to remember this other kind of knowledge and love, which has forever been a way of reaching complexes of emotion and relationship, the attitude that is like the attitude of science and the other arts today, but with significant and beautiful distinctness from these—the attitude that perhaps might equip our imaginations to deal with our lives—the attitude of poetry.

What help is there here?

Poetry is, above all, an approach to the truth of feeling, and what is the use of truth?

How do we use feeling?

How do we use truth?

However confused the scene of our life appears, however torn we may be who now do face that scene, it can be faced, and we can go on to be whole.

If we use the resources we now have, we and the world itself may move in one fullness. Moment to moment, we can grow, if we can bring ourselves to meet the moment with our lives.

To do this, we need to understand our resources and ourselves. In a time of suffering, long war, and the opening of the horizon, there is no resource which we can afford to overlook or to misunderstand.

Coming to this moment, at which the great religious ideas become in a new way available to everyone, one enters a climate of possibility. And in that air, in time of struggle, and in time of the idea of the world, all people think about love. Then they turn to their own ways of sharing.

In speaking about poetry, I must say at the beginning that the subject has no acknowledged place in American life today.

No matter how deeply one is concerned with poetry, the feeling against it is likely to be an earlier one to most of us. In approaching the subject, it may have more realities to us if we look first, not at poetry itself, but at the resistances to poetry.

Each of us will recognize this resistance in his own life. The barriers that have been set up are strong; this is nothing that enters our lives, in social life as it is now organized.

Certain of our resources are good indexes to all the rest. There are relationships which include so much that we can bring to them our own wishes and hostilities, our value judgments and our moralities; they will serve to illuminate all our other relationships. Among them are such key targets for our attitudes as conflict in the individual, the atom bomb, the Negroes, the Reds, the Jews, the "place" of science, the "place" of labor, the "place" of women, and poetry. These points are crucial; our age and our nature find that questions are asked of them.

Now poetry, at this moment, stands in curious relationship to our acceptance of life and our way of living.

The resistance to poetry is an active force in American life during these wars. Poetry is not; or seems not to be. But it appears that among the great conflicts of this culture, the conflict in our attitude toward poetry stands clearly lit. There are no guards built up to hide it. We can see its expression, and we can see its effects upon us. We can see our own conflict and our own resource if we look, now, at this art, which has been made—of all the arts—the one least acceptable.

Anyone dealing with poetry and the love of poetry must deal, then, with the hatred of poetry, and perhaps even more with the indifference which is driven toward the center. It comes through as boredom, as name-calling, as the traditional attitude of the last hundred years which has chalked in the portrait of the poet as he is known to this society, which, as Herbert Read says, "does not challenge poetry in principle—it merely treats it with ignorance, indifference and unconscious cruelty."

Poetry is foreign to us, we do not let it enter our daily lives.

Do you remember the poems of your early childhood—the

far rhymes and games of the beginning to which you called the rhythms, the little songs to which you woke and went to sleep?

Yes, we remember them.

But since childhood, to many of us poetry has become a matter of distaste. The speaking of poetry is one thing: one of the qualifications listed for an announcer on a great network, among "good voice" and "correct pronunciation," is the "ability to read and interpret poetry." The other side is told conclusively in a letter sent ninety years ago by the wife of the author of *Moby-Dick*. Mrs. Melville said to her mother— "Herman has taken to writing poetry. You need not tell anyone, for you know how such things get around."

What is the nature of this distaste?

If you ask your friends about it, you will find that there are a few answers, repeated by everyone. One is that the friend has not the *time* for poetry. This is a curious choice, since poetry, of all the arts that live in time—music, theater, film, writing—is the briefest, the most compact. Or your friends may speak of their boredom with poetry. If you hear this, ask further. You will find that "boredom" is a masking answer, concealing different meanings. One person will confess that he has been frightened off forever by the dry dissection of lines in school, and that now he thinks with disappointment of a poem as simply a set of constructions. He expects much more. One will say that he returned from the scenes of war to a high-school classroom reading "Bobolink, bobolink / Spink, spank, spink." A first-rate scientist will search for the formal framework of the older poetry in despair, and finally stop. One will confess that, try as he will, he cannot understand poetry, and more particularly, modern writing. It is intellectual, confused, unmusical. One will say it is willfully obscure. One that it is inapplicable to the situation in which he finds himself. And almost any man will say that it is effeminate: it is true that poetry as an art is sexually suspect.

In all of these answers, we meet a slipping-away which is the clue to the responses, and which is strong enough to be called more than direct resistance.

This resistance has the quality of fear, it expresses the fear of poetry.

I have found in working with people and with poems, that this fear presents the symptoms of a psychic problem. A poem does invite, it does require. What does it invite? A poem invites you to feel. More than that: it invites you to respond. And better than that: a poem invites a total response.

This response is total, but it is reached through the emotions. A fine poem will seize your imagination intellectually—that is, when you reach it, you will reach it intellectually too—but the way is through emotion, through what we call feeling.

PROCESS AND RELATIONSHIP

The angry things that have been said about our poetry have also been said about our time. They are both "confused," "chaotic," "violent," "obscure."

There is a clue here, and it is more than a reflection. It is not that an art "reflects," as the schoolbooks say, an age. But in the relationship may be a possible answer, a possible direction.

The illumination will lie in the relationship itself.

One way to look at scientific material, or the data of human life, is fact by fact, deriving the connections.

Another way, more fruitful I believe, is to look at the relationships themselves, learning the facts as they feed or destroy each other. When we see that, we will see whether they tend toward an equilibrium, or strain spent on war away, or be poised at the rare moment of balance.

I think of the work of Willard Gibbs in science.

Or of Karen Horney in psychoanalysis, here: defining action in terms of relationship, so that the individual is seen not only as an individual, but as a person moving toward other persons, or a person moving away from other persons, or a person moving against other persons.

And I think of a scene at the Rockefeller Institute I saw: the rabbit, its great thrust and kick of muscular pride, as it was carried under the fluorescent lights, where against the colored unbroken skin glowed the induced cancers, fluorescing violet. A research doctor had come up from Johns Hopkins to talk to a biophysicist working in ways resembling his own. And in the basement lab, with its tubes, its beakers, its electrophoresis setup, he told how the work he was doing in cancer had changed in its nature, in its meaning. His colleagues and himself were no longer looking at cancer as a fact, an isolated fact.

They were taking another approach: they were dealing with cancer and the body on which it fed as one thing—an equilibrium which had been set up, in which the cancer fed on the host. One could not exist in this state without the other in that state. It was the relationship which was the illness. And he felt that these terms led to the right questions.

When we talk about relationships in art, we can see at once how all kinds of activity have taken this direction. The work of Freud and Picasso and Einstein are familiar to us as the masterwork in relative values, in the search for individual maturity, in visual imagination, in physical science; Joyce we recognize as working in the relationships of language, Marx in social relationship from which the fact could be derived—and these are the key names alone, in a few fields.

In our own time, we have become used to an idea of history in which process and relationship are stressed. The science of ecology is only one example of an elaboration of the idea, so that the life of land may be seen in terms of its tides of growth, the feeding of one group on another, the equilibrium reached, broken, and the drive toward another balance and renewal.

We think of the weather now as a dance of airs, predictable in relationship, with its parades of clouds, the appetites of pressure areas, and aftermath of foreseen storms.

But in the areas dealing with emotion and belief, there is hesitation. The terms have not been invented; and although that does not impede expressive writing—a poem, a novel, or a play *act emotions out* in terms of words, they do not describe—the lack does impede analytical work. We have no terms, for example, for "emotional meaning" or "emotional information." We have not even the English for Claude Bernard's "*milieu intérieur,*" that internal condition of a body, the *in*vironment where live the inner relationships.

That obstacle is nothing.

We are poets; we can make the words.

The emotional obstacle is the real one.

For the question is asked in a thousand ways each day: Is poetry alive? Is there a place for poetry? What is that place?

NOT TO BE USED

In our schools, we are told that our education is pragmatic, that the body of knowledge is divided into various "subjects," that all of these subjects on which we pour our youth are valuable and useful to us in later life. We are told that our civilization depends on further and new uses for everything it has, the development and exploitation of these. We may go ahead and specialize in any of these usable fields.

Except for one.

There is one *kind* of knowledge that will be given to us all through school and high school, which we are told is precious, it defies time, it strikes deep into memory, it must go on being taught. No matter what cities fall, what languages are mis-heard and "corrupted" and reborn. This is here, to be passed on. But not to be used. Among all this pragmatic training, never to come into the real and active life.

That is what we learn about poetry.

THE KING-KILLERS

I remember a psychologist with whom I talked in New Haven. That is a good town to produce an image of the split life: it is a split town, part fierce industrial city, part college, very little reconciled—and in the center of the town, on the Green, is a symbol which is as good as any for this meaning. On the New Haven Green, itself a hub of tradition, there is a church which is old, respected, well-proportioned and serene. Down to its cornerstones: but these stones, these stones are set up as monuments to two of the English regicides who escaped to America after the Restoration. Two of the men who killed King Charles. A church founded on the stones of king-killers, men who broke the most extreme of taboos! But that is the gesture, the violent axiom-breaking gesture of the imagination that takes its side, chooses its tradition and sets to work.

In such a town, I spoke to a psychologist, a man who has made his work and his theme the study of fear, and the talk went well enough until poetry was mentioned. Then, with extreme violence, a violence out of any keeping with what had gone before, the psychologist began to raise his voice and cut the air with his hand flat. He said, his voice shaking, that he had cut poetry out of his life, that that was something he had not time for, that was something out of his concern.

I have thought of him often.

His attitude is the attitude of the schools. It is widespread now;

but the symbol of the church is, I think, closer to our people. I choose it and I speak for it.

THE PEOPLE WHO RULE OUT POETRY

I speak against the fear that rules out poetry. It seems to me that this fear of poetry is against all imagination and the work that is closest to imagination: experiment in human relation, religious exploration, political novelty, "abstract" art, abstract science. The people who feel that work in these fields is dangerous, a threat, give evidence of what has broken down.

They are also the people who say that in Europe they see nothing but confusion, in China they see nothing but confusion; and there is nothing but confusion at home.

They are our next reactionaries, who will admit only confusion wherever there are new forces trying to express their direction. But that is another matter, one of which I will speak later.

If the difficulty that they indicate is truly there—if communication has broken down, then it is time to tap the roots of communication.

Poetry is written from these depths; in great poetry you feel a source speaking to another source.

And it is deep at these levels that the questions lie.

They come up again and again during these years, when under all the surface shouting, there is silence about those things we need to hear.

WHAT SHOULD I BE FEELING?

The fear that cuts off poetry is profound: it plunges us deep, far back to the edge of childhood. Beyond that it does not go.

Little children do not have this fear, they trust their emotions. But on the threshold of adolescence the walls are built.

Against the assaults of puberty, and in those silvery delicate seasons when all feeling casts about for confirmation. Then, for the first time, you wonder "What should I be feeling?" instead of the true "What do you feel?" "What do I feel?" Now the easily talented and the easily skillful are loved in classrooms and the field.

It takes a great pressure behind an adolescent wish to make it persist through all the change of growth.

The first stoppage of expression becomes final here, a malignant process may now begin. If you visit these rooms, you will see it happen, the wonder dried out of a passage read and re-read aloud for emphasis; the stories undercut by parsings and explanations, often for language alone, the shell of language, seldom for meaning.

Grammar and criticism need not destroy; but they will, if words are raised above language, if criticism is projected by the critic's lack, if a dry perfectionism is substituted for the creative life.

You will remember the times: were you the high-school junior in the streetcar who shook his head—No—when you were asked, half in contempt, half in the hope of another answer—"Do you read poetry?"

In adults, you know those who put poetry far behind them; not naturally, like children outgrowing toys who forget them (or beat them to pieces), but with a painful shocked awareness that here was something outside their reach. It would be all right, because society likes that attitude; however, neurotically, they call attention to it still. More than one editor, introducing his anthology, will confess that poetry is something he "knows nothing about"; there are reviewers who will go glibly on about any kind of novel or first biography, but who write uneasily, in language as clumsy as the first page of a diary, whenever they face a book of poems.

WASTE, AND THE EMOTIONAL LIFE

If we have a resource that we are not using…

If this were a crop, about which these things were said, there would be a research project.

If it were a metal, the Un-American Activities Committee, and several other committees, would concern themselves. Our scientists would claim their right of experiment and inquiry.

There are many causes for waste in our life. We are very sure of ourselves in some powers and wildly insecure in others: the imbalance leads to random action, waste, hostilities out of reason. Margaret Mead describes us as a "third generation" society. She does not mean, of course, that we are all the grandchildren of pioneers and immigrants; but she does mean that our parents shared the attitudes of the children of foreigners, who because of their strange families, with their old-country ways, their effusive gestures, the flavor of their speech, leaned over backward to rule out any foreignness, any color at all.

We suffer from that background, with its hunger for uniformity, the shared norm of ambition and habit and living standard. The repressive codes are everywhere. Our movies are censored before they are plotted; our radio comedy is forbidden its list of themes; have you noticed how our bestselling books are written in reaction to the dominating woman?

This code strikes deep at our emotional life.

Its action means that our emotions are supposed to be uniform. Since that is impossible, our weaknesses send us to meet any divergence from the expected with dread or conflict.

This leads on the one hand to the immense incidence of "mental" disease which we find in America now; and, on the other, I believe we may say that it leads to a fear of poetry.

Our education is one of specialization. We become experts in some narrow "field." That expertness allows us to deal with the limited problems presented to us; it allows us to face emotional reality, symbolic reality, very little. That can be seen very clearly in our movies, which now will use clever methods to imitate reality—in one battle film, the cameraman shook his camera at the moment of explosion, so that an entire scene would shake—Hollywood movies have absorbed documentary methods, and have then stopped just short of reality, or of creating an arrangement by which a movie can give us a sense of reality. A first-rate scientist, or a fine prose writer, is able to say "How can I know a good poem? I can tell an honest piece of work in my own field from a phony piece of work, but how can I tell a fine poem from a phony poem?" And what has to be said to such a question is that these are people who cannot trust their emotional reactions, their total reactions.

They are people who are insecure enough not to trust themselves when images are related to images and emotions to emotions.

One characteristic of modern poetry is that arrangement of parts which strikes many people as being violent or obscure. It is a method which is familiar enough on the screen; when you see the picture of a nightclub, and then see the heroine's face thrown back as she sings, you make the unity without any effort, without even being conscious of your process.

There is no confusion for you, partly because the eye is selective in just these ways; that is the arrangement according to which you see the room you were in yesterday and this book against the wall or floor, with a practiced change of focus, with much skill at putting together the "information" your eyes provide you. It is the way you look at the scene before you, and it is also the sequence in which you very likely "see" your dreams.

Now films and visual sequences may be put together smoothly with all the links filled in, or according to other rhythms, in which one sequence will approach a main meaning, to be cut off by another sequence—about different people, in different circumstances, say—so that the third sequence will be reinforced, made to change and grow because of what has gone before.

Much of modern poetry moves in terms of quick, rhythmic juxtapositions. Our contemporary journalism still uses more even linkage. Each method prepares you for the climaxes of the poem. If you can be flexible of mind, remembering movies you have liked, and being aware of their richness and suspense and the dense texture of their realities, you are approaching what may have seemed to you the most broken of modern poetry.

Using these ways of bringing-together, these arrangements, we find more often that our poems are not lyrics or one-emotion poems. The lyric, like

> *Cherry-ripe, ripe, ripe, I cry,*
> *Full and fair ones; come and buy.*
> *If so be you ask me where*
> *They do grow, I answer: There*
> *Where my Julia's lips do smile;...*

may be illustrated by the diagram of a point moving from A to B, to C, to D, to E.

The poems which depend on several emotions, each carrying its images, move like a cluster traveling from one set of positions to another: the group $ABCDE$, say, moving to $A'B'C'D'E'$; a constellation.

This gathering-together of elements so that they move together according to a newly visible system is becoming evident in all our sciences, and it is natural that it should be present in our writing. Wherever it exists, it gives us a clue as to a possible kind of imagination with which to meet the world. It gives us a clue that may lead to a way to deal with any unity which depends on many elements, all inter-dependent.

THE MEANINGS OF POETRY

I have invoked the meanings of poetry as they help to clear us and make whole the spirit. We can make the connections, and loose the combining force. There are great gashes in our world that we love with so much pain. Deep gashes we all receive; the ones who foresee them, and the ones who live through them once, when they arrive. Gashes are inflicted on our awareness very early, and we recognize them when we see children dancing or making their songs, when we find primitive peoples in their religion, their poetry, their ability to dance their shared foreboding.

Much of that has been taken away from us; but now we need to look for the relating forces. The forces, that is, that love to make and perceive relationships and cause them to grow; they may be most complex.

As poetry is complex.

For poetry, in the sense in which I am using the word, is very like the love of which Diotima told Socrates. She, speaking of love, told how it was of its nature neither good nor beautiful, for its desire was the beautiful, its desire was the good.

I speak, then, of a poetry which tends *where form tends, where meanings tend*.

This will be a poetry which is concerned with the crises of our spirit, with the music and the images of these meanings. It will also be a poetry of meeting-places, where the false barriers go down. For they are false.

THE INVITATION

During the war, we felt the silence in the policy of the governments of English-speaking countries. That policy was to win the war first, and work out the meanings afterward. The result was, of course, that the meanings were lost. You cannot put these things off.

One of the invitations of poetry is to come to the emotional meanings at every moment. That is one reason for the high concentration of music, in poetry.

The putting-off of meaning has already been reflected in the fashionable writing of the last years. Our most popular novels and poems have been works of easy mysticism or easy wit, with very little between. One entire range is represented, for us, in the literature of aversion. There has been much silence.

The silence of fear. Of the impoverished imagination, which avoids, and makes a twittering, and is still.

Communication comes, to make this place fertile, to make it possible to meet the world with all the resources we have, the fund of faith, the generous instruments of imagination and knowledge.

Poetry may be seen as one sum of such equipment, as an image of the kind of fullness that can best meet the evening, the hostile imagination—which restricts, denies, and proclaims death—and the inner clouds which mask our fears.

Now we turn to memory, we search all the days we had forgotten for a tradition that can support our arms in such a moment. If we are free people, we are also in a sense free to choose our past, at every moment to choose the tradition we will bring to the future. We invoke a rigorous positive, that will enable us to imagine our choices, and to make them.

Is it possible that the "chaos" of our time and the "obscurity" that labels our poetry have a common base—that there are clusters of events and emotions which require new ways of making them more human, and that modern art and modern science have a clue to provide?

Is there a common denominator here? What possible "exercise" can the emotions find, what possible freeing of emotion is there, that can train us to face the immediate future?

CHAPTER TWO

THE UNIVERSE OF POETRY

There has been a failure between poetry and its people—its writers and audience. There are two frameworks here, two universes, as the algebras define the term. There is the universe of poetry and the universe of non-poetry. Between music and non-music there is an outlying district, a buffer, a slum of the "semi-classical." There is some of that in verse, of course; too much; but the areas here are more sharply defined light and dark.

It is not alone that we have failed poetry.

Poetry has failed us too. It has not been good enough. We want this voice now, we want voices to speak to us as we move, directly, insisting on full consciousness. What truth does this lead to, at its best?

The universe of poetry is the universe of emotional truth.

Our material is the way we feel and the way we remember.

A HISTORY OF IMAGES

Now very little is known of these. We are able to judge from action—and this includes the making and receiving of art—*what* is being felt, and we know to a certain extent *what* is remembered. We are able sometimes to trace the stimulus.

But here the artist has often set the problem. In tracing the connection between art and science, we see that the flow is as often from art as toward it. Proust is one of the pioneers of the memory, and his problem is only now beginning to be taken up by the psychiatrists and the mathematicians.

The history of our emotional meanings is everywhere acted out: in the images which cities are, in all our buildings and decorations, in our greetings and our dance, our music. It is made plain in speech.

And, lacking the record of dream, we have something more, in our writing.

Look at a transcript of any psychoanalysis. You will find raw imagery in the river of the patient's speech, raw suffering, the puns and repetition and new words of the turned-in invalid who is not yet beginning to hope, who has begun only to remember and describe.

But the order, the music, has been thrown away.

AN AGE OPENING

There are many people who will say that this is not a time for poetry.

It is a fact that there is little enough to which anyone can point and say, "That poem speaks to me."

They will speak of Elizabethan England as the great setting for poets. There was a sense, then, they will tell you, of expansion and discovery unlimited—of the new and the strange within reach—the hostile legendary seas now opening upon other countries under God, with striped men, greenness beyond imagined jungles, every monster newness, volcanoes of gold; a swarm to the mind, so that it must open, go it must and discover. All appetite and power is suddenly here, within the hand, within the poem, to those who dare.

Mostly because of two things: the sea, sea-power, what that meant to the island, and because of that most excellent invention, America.

Our age is opening now. We have the air, and its other dimension. We have the frontier of nuclear energy, whose curse has already been chosen, and for whose blessing we must live. And we have, for the first time in history, among all the longing for communication which we can see everywhere: communication with the secret life of the individual, communication through machines, communication between peoples—we have the sense of the world—a real and spiritual unity which offers greater newness than America, greater explorations, and wealth of human meanings and resources that has never before been reached.

We have, in the opening of such a time, a sense of an age disclosing undefined possibilities, new meanings for multiplicity, and new meanings for unity.

This age contains the promise of poetry among its great promises.

But this is simply one of many needs.

ART IN LIFE

Poetry will not answer these needs. It is art: it imagines and makes, and gives you the imaginings. Because you have imagined love, you have not loved; merely because you have imagined brotherhood, you have not made brotherhood. You may feel as though you had, but you have not. You are going to have to use that imagining as you best can, by building it into yourself, or you will be left with nothing but illusion.

Art is action, but it does not cause action: rather, it prepares us for thought.

Art is intellectual, but it does not cause thought: rather, it prepares us for thought.

Art is not a world, but a knowing of the world. Art prepares us.

Art is practiced by the artist and the audience. It is not a means to an end, unless that end is the total imaginative experience.

That experience will have meaning. It will apply to your life; and it is more than likely to lead you to thought or action, that is, you are likely to want to go further into the world, further into yourself, toward further experience.

THE USABLE TRUTH

Art and nature are imitations, not of each other, but of the same third thing—both images of the real, the spectral and vivid reality that employs all means. If we fear it in art, we fear it in nature, and our fear brings it on ourselves in the most unanswerable ways.

The implications for society and for the individual are far-reaching.

People want this speech, this immediacy. They need it. The fear of poetry is a complicated and civilized repression of that need. We wish to be told, in the most memorable way, what we have been meaning all along.

This is a ritual moment, a moment of proof.

We need all our implements, and there is strength in these moments.

All the equipment of tradition and invention offers us access to this door, and they work against the totalitarian hardening of modern life as it expresses itself in the state. There is an entire line for us to choose: there is no poetic science, but there are pillars, there are clues. Whitman, one answers, Melville. Melville has given us a challenge which could stand as the core of a tradition, in a phrase hard-headed enough for the most Yankee. He speaks it in a moving and potent letter:

"There is a certain tragic phase of humanity which, in our

opinion, was never more powerfully embodied than by Hawthorne. We mean the tragedies of human thought in its own unbiased, native, and profounder workings. We think that into no recorded mind has the intense feeling of the usable truth ever entered more deeply than into this man's. By usable truth, we mean the apprehension of the absolute condition of present things as they strike the eye of the man who fears them not, though they do their worst to him,—the man who, like Russia or the British Empire, declares himself a sovereign nature (in himself) amid the powers of heaven, hell, and earth. He may perish; but so long as he exists he insists on treating with all powers upon an equal basis. If any of those other Powers choose to withhold certain secrets, let them; that does not impair my sovereignty in myself; that does not make me tributary. And perhaps, after all, there is *no* secret...."

That pride is deep in our meaning, and in our truth.

But what use is there? What is the use of truth? Is not truth the end? Or has it no human use, does it lead to nothing?

The use of truth is its communication.

CHAPTER THREE

THE SECURITY OF THE IMAGINATION

It used to be agreed that painting was a visual, music an auditory art. R. G. Collingwood, in his brilliant *The Principles of Art*, goes on to tell how Cézanne came then, and began to paint like a blind man. His rooms are full of volumes: these tables, the people in these chairs are bulks which have been felt with the hands. These trees are not what trees look like, they are what trees feel like. And Mont Saint-Victoire is over one's head, rearing in voluntary power like Wordsworth's mountain.

Impossible it was to reach poetry according to the old aesthetic. A break was made between spoken poetry and written poetry. The function of the poet—whether he was heard, read, or for that matter, forgotten—entered the argument and complicated its error. For the fact is that painting is not a visual art. A painting is made by the hands of the painter, setting up the imaginative experience taken through his eyes. Music is written by the hand of the composer, giving us the imaginative experience through the ears. Poetry is made by the hand of the poet, and if we read the poem, we take the imaginative experience through the eyes with a *shadow* of sound; if we hear it, we take it through the ears with a *shadow* of sight.

Limits may be set on this by work with the illiterate, the blind and the deaf, who can help us to know the ways of sense.

But the reality of all the arts is that of the imagination.

The fear of poetry is an indication that we are cut off from our own reality.

All of our nature must be used. It is fatal now to hold back from it. The war that has been over the world was a war made in our imaginations; we saw it coming, and said so; and our imaginations must be strong enough to make a peace. First, to create an idea of that peace, and then to bring it about.

Always we need the audacity to speak for more freedom, more imagination, more poetry with all its meanings. As we go deeper into conflict, we shall find ourselves more constrained, the repressive codes will turn to iron. More and more we shall need to be free in our beliefs, as we come to our forms.

The question of form and technique rises here. In art we recognize that within this constraint is our discovery. Necessity is indeed the source of freedom. But many readers think of form in poetry as a framework. It is not that. The form and music of the fine poems are organic, they are not frames. They follow the laws of organic growth in ways I shall attempt to show.

There has been a great deal of political talk about security in this century. Growth is the security of organic life. The security of the imagination lies in calling, all our lives, for more liberty, more rebellion, more belief.

As far as we do that, our culture is alive.

Those who speak of our culture as dead or dying have a quarrel with life, and I think they cannot understand its terms, but must endlessly repeat the projection of their own despair.

The even pitch of life and culture is not our scene. The moment of great height, of infinite depth, is here. There is a famous passage in the works of the great imaginative scientist,

James Clerk Maxwell, in which he draws attention to the implications of what are called in mathematics "singular points." A stone poised on another stone, a ball rolling in perfect motion on a perfect wedge, a supersaturated solution, are examples, and the equations for their systems break down at these extraordinary moments in their history. Clerk Maxwell believed that the science of the future would be deeply concerned with these crises in "systems of high rank." We may be said to be living in a system which has reached such a point.

Unless you share such conception, you will be likely to see what is happening as "confusion"; to say with one that culture is dying in a shift of powers, or with another that we have lost the way and must live as well as we can.

The way is before us, and culture is the future as well as the past.

Time in culture is capable of many arrangements. Dante read today sets up different relations, very likely, from Dante read in his own decades, but the change is not in Dante nor in his truth, although many will say so. These truths, the truth of the voyage, of the skull-grinding horror, the white chance, leopard, star, and belief, are present. There is no particular question of death, since we are in a life where imaginative experience is given and taken.

Choose your poet here. Or, rather, do not choose. But remember what happened to you when you came to your poem, any poem whose truth overcame all inertia in you at that moment, so that your slow mortality took its proper place, and before it the light of a new awareness was not something new, but something you *recognized*.

That is the multiple time-sense in poetry, that is the ever new, which is recognized as something already in ourselves, but not discovered.

That moment of impact may reach you on a first reading of

a poem. It may not arrive until a fifth or sixth reading. A student rebelling against a first poem of Gerard Manley Hopkins said of "The Windhover": "I read it and hated it. It seemed a thick, stuttering, un-understandable thing. I like piano music, and I play the piano. It seemed to me there was no music here that I could grasp. But I had been told to read this poem several times, and I did it—four or five readings, angrier each time. I felt very irritated and tired, and fell asleep. When I woke in the morning, I thought of the poem at once. The book was still open, and I read 'The Windhover.' It leapt into place, clearly and in a purity of speech and music I had never known before. I knew things I had not suspected, but in a strange way, like remembering."

It is difficult to report that kind of experience. There is danger of its sounding like a clumsy testimonial. But that danger is like the one involved in telling about religious experience, which has many similarities; and the awkwardness is one that comes in a moment of truth, when the unaccustomed spirit puts off clothes and is naked; and there is a beginning like the beginning of a dance.

Not only the truth of the poem has been reached.

It would be better to say that the truth of the poem is the truth both of the poet and the reader. It has been given and taken.

It is an emotional and imaginative truth. Very little yet is known about its laws and functions.

But that is the deep life of poetry.

It is reflecting your lives.

GESTURE AND IMAGE

Now there are gestures in our lives that stand in direct relationship to the image in poetry.

The meanings of poetry take their growth through the interaction of the images and the music of the poem. The music is not the rhythm, which is a representation of life, alone. The music involves the interplay of the sounds of words, the length of sequences, the keeping and breaking of rhythms, and the repetition and variation of syllables unrhymed and rhymed. It also involves the play of ideas and images.

The statement of ideas in a poem may have to do with logic. More profoundly, it may be identified with the emotional progression of the poem, in terms of the music and images, so that the poem is alive throughout.

Another, more fundamental statement in poetry, is made through the images themselves—those declarations, evocative, exact, and musical, which move through time and are the actions of a poem.

The poetic image is not a static thing. It lives in time, as does the poem. Unless it is the first image of the poem, it has already been prepared for by other images; and it prepares us for further images and rhythms to come. Even if it is the first image of the poem, the establishment of the rhythm prepares us—musically— for the music of the image. And if its first word begins the poem, it has the role of putting into motion all the course of images and music of the entire work, with nothing to refer to, except perhaps a title.

If we look at a few images that open their poems, these descriptions will at once be plain:

Give me my scallop-shell of quiet,

sets the song-rhythm, the scene of a palmer's journey, and the tone of spiritual necessity, which Raleigh's "The Passionate Man's Pilgrimage" carries through the lyric.

They flee from me, that sometime did me seek,
With naked foot stalking in my chamber:

impels Sir Thomas Wyatt's poem, "They flee from me…" in two lines, deep into its long-cadenced music and all the nighttime, bitter and regretful change.

A modern opening, that of Crane's "The Broken Tower," may be analyzed further. The first image dispatches, not only the "me" of the poem, but the poem itself:

> *The bell-rope that gathers God at dawn*
> *Dispatches me as though I dropped down the knell*
> *Of a spent day—*

and the ringing irregular sway of the poem, its "steps from hell," the hiving of the stars and the broken world, follow until the tower becomes flesh and word; until the lake and tower of the ending take on their full meaning after many reverberations, sound after sound and image after image hunting back—not only to the beginning, but to each successive image and each successive sequence of sound.

The images of a poem have so curious a motion. This is certainly more apparent in a short poem—one of the length, say, of "The Broken Tower," which can be held easily by the memory or the page. (It occupies two pages as I have it in print before me; to scan the full effect, I suggest you copy it out so that you can have it all on a sheet.) The relationships in sound are dense in the first stanza: "The bell-rope" evoking the syllables in "dispatches," "dropped down the knell," "spent day," "pit to crucifix," "feet chill on steps from hell." "Gathers" turns us back to "rope" in the novelty of its idea of the bell-rope gathering God; "dawn" and "spent day" set up a ripple of context, and "dispatches" and "dropped down" tie both idea and music more tightly to the meaning.

One cannot say, of course, tie both idea and music more

tightly to the meaning. The idea, the music, and the meaning are identified. Nothing here is "tied." The bonds are those of imaginative and musical relationship. I use the word "bonds," and think of the disappointment of Orpheus before the sibyl, to whom he went in mourning, for an oracle. The sibyl said only:

The Furies are the bonds of men

giving to Orpheus an unsuspected presage of his death, and speaking of the ties that at once chain and connect human beings.

The bonds of poetry, which make for form and development, are those of growth within the poem. And if the poem grows by means of its images, what do these images resemble and reflect in our lives?

JOHN BROWN, CAROSSA, AND SOME OTHERS

It seems to me that the gestures we may compare are the images of history, and those symbols which carry through many levels of training and background to reach us imaginatively. Certain lives do that, so that the whole life becomes an image reaching backward and forward in history, illuminating all time. The life of Jesus; the life of Buddha; the life of Lincoln, or Gandhi, or Saint Francis—these give us the intensity that should be felt in a lifetime of concentration, a lifetime which seems to risk the immortal meanings every day, pure in knowledge that the only way to realize them is to risk them. Think, too, of Beethoven's life, of the Curies and Father Damien; or of that living person whose daily meanings carry most to you. These lives, in their search and purpose, offer their form, offer their truths. They reach us as hope.

At the "singular points" in history—to return to Clerk Maxwell's phrase—certain gestures provide expression. Heroes are made. That is, a man or woman allows many people to feel the moment of crisis, and to understand that it is common to all imaginations ready to receive its meaning.

In this country, one man who cut through to the imagination of all was John Brown, that meteor, whose blood was love and rage, in fury until the love was burned away. That crazy murderous old man, he must be called by Lincoln, and he must be hanged, condemned in agony. But that precipitating stroke, like the archaic bloody violence of the Greek plays, spoke to many lives.

In Denmark, during the last war, the Jews were required by edict to wear the yellow Star of David which would mark them and set them apart. On the first day of the edict's validity, nobody appeared in the street without the yellow badge. In a great simple act of love and identification, the Danish people had canceled the power of a ruling that, without the acceptance of the majority, could not force any group apart from the rest of the people.

And in fascist Germany, one first-rate poet stayed. He was rumored by the exiles to be one thing and another. He was a man of good will, a doctor and a poet, who had written, all his life, against war and against the masks of evil, saying, "God give us each his sin to awaken him!" Now he was writing the poems of the newborn, and myths of many returnings, of the pure coming home, stronger, more beautiful than before, after destruction. He was reading publicly, to the Hitler Youth; and a storm of hatred arose from his old friends. He did accept, it was true, the invitations that others refused in pride. He did go and read, to packed meetings; and what he said in his defense was "I cannot withhold my gentle voice." He was against them, and they wanted him. They seemed to want what he had to say. The offering of his parables, his gentleness that allowed himself to give these words of renewal and peace to whomever asked them of him—they are part of a gesture which, I believe, reaches softly and graciously to the imagination.

These gestures speak to many lives. They give hope and impetus to many kinds of people.

They are infinitely multiplied. You will know those who risked themselves and died in the Resistance movements of many lands; little children, who in a far-reaching moment of consciousness, made their gifts; miners, anonymous women, those suffering and poor, and the privileged of all functions in life, those gifted with insight so that they understand the beauty of unconditional love, and live and make their gifts. The gestures of the individuals are not history; but they are the images of history.

TWO SYMBOLS

There are old symbols which have persisted among many tribes, as there are myths which may seem to us to have been dreamed privately at night, until we find them recurring in many literatures as stories and magic lore. One such symbol is the swastika, the sign of direction, of the guardianship of the season-ruling gods, and of birth. Another even older one is the spiral, the life-giver and carrier, the whirlpool, the vortex of atoms, and the sacred circuit.

Some theories of the origin of symbols hold that such symbols were "natural" decorative art, an "art motif" which pleased the fancy, which "went well." Other theories stress the idea of luck, or say that "savages" simply "filled in" their significant designs with these forms.

Donald A. Mackenzie, in his study of the two symbols, speaks savagely of these theories, citing example after example of their value and asking at one point why, if it was merely "pretty," was it incised on the inner stone of a tomb, concealed, and left for the soul to find and admire, exclaiming, "Pretty!"

"Ancient religious art," Mackenzie says, "invariably expressed something by means of its symbols." The cross and the swastika were not imitative, like the representations of wings or horns; they were expressions of ideas.

The spiral, which began by being imitative—the form is, of course, found countlessly in nature (in ivy, in water, in hair, in shells, ears, whirlwinds)—and went on to be associated with a process. The symbol then asked the question, or declared the existence of the problem of the relationship of movement with life. The magic and energy spirals, Kundalini the coiled serpent, the pearl spiral of Yang, are connected in meaning and form. The wheel of birth and the spiral nebula of Democritus—long before the nebula could be seen through a lens—preceded by the lengths of many cultures our watch-spring spirals and logarithmic spirals.

Where ancient man made his connections, identifying "trees and stones, horns and pillars and mountains, rivers, lakes and heavenly bodies," because all were parts of a perfect whole—in these same forms, modern man reads the relative velocities of growth. He sees the distinction between other forms in nature, of which no one part is older than any other, and this spiral horn or shell, which keeps all the stages of its growth, which belongs to the living, yet is not alive, remain in being incapable of change. He sees how "in the equiangular spiral *the time element* always enters in"—this is Sir D'Arcy Wentworth Thompson—and he calculates the imaginary contract-spiral, the growth of generating curves, and the vector rotation of planes.

The history of a symbol, traced in this way, will show the history of human passion for a relationship—in this instance, between growth and form. Passion it is, deeper, more eager to use and be used, and in its love and play making art, games, talismans, out of an expression of the most deep connection.

As the symbol is the dramatic element of religion—and the symbol is the expression of a distinct relationship between sacred energy and the human being—so is the gesture the dramatic element of history. The image is the dramatic element of poetry. It is contained in the gross dramatic action of a poem, in which the characters act out their meaning. In the image, a relationship of language acts out its meaning.

A poem is not its images any more than a symphony is its themes.

A poem is not its words any more than a symphony is its notes.

The image, the word, the note—those are methods by which the imaginative experience is presented and received.

"The image," says C. Day Lewis in *The Poetic Image*, "is a method of asserting or reasserting spiritual control over the material." And he makes a very suggestive definition of what the critics have called "pure poetry" as "poetry whose meaning is deliberately concentrated within its images."

But behind these notions of control lies, every time, belief.

Faith is found here, not in a destiny raiding and parcelling out knowledge and the earth, but in a people who, person by person, believes itself. Do you accept your own gestures and symbols? Do you believe what you yourself say? When you act, do you believe what you are doing?

It comes to that, if form is going to be achieved in life or art; although that is only the beginning. Profound and ironic honesty, that tests itself, that stays alert and sensitive. But we cannot stop here; if we settle for honesty, we are selling out.

Much more is needed before imagination can make its gifts. The form and content have not yet reached their true level, where one is a function of the other.

In poetry, form and content, relation and function, reach and merge.

In history, the form and content of beliefs are not like Yang and Yin, one all dark one all bright, they cannot be set against one another. They merge, and the vanquished in war may still, years later, invade the fears of a victor nation. The content of faith, for us, is not opposite to, exclusive of, other faiths. The whirlwinds of the North circle this way; south of the Equator they drive eternally *against*. With the form the same, direction is the factor of distinction.

The form of their belief marked those in Denmark that day, all the underground fighters, the savage and gentle heroes of our long way. At the same time, that form evoked its comparable belief in countless lives.

These men and women express connection. That is their gift in life, as it is the gift of art.

The knowledge of this gift is very powerful.

The uses of such knowledge are wide; its ignorance is fatal.

This is one skill we have not used, reaching that makes a meeting-place.

Facing and communicating, that will be our life, in the world and in poetry. Are we to teach this? All we can show to people is themselves; show them what passion they possess, and we will all have come to the poetry. This is the knowledge of communication, and it is the fear of it which has cut us down.

Our lives may rest on this; and our lives are our images.

CHAPTER FOUR

TOWARD THE MOST HUMAN; INTENSITY WITHIN FORM

If our imaginative response to life were complete, if we were fully conscious of emotion, if we apprehended surely the relations that make us know the truth and the relations that make us know the beautiful, we would be—what? The heroes of our myths, acting perfectly among these faculties, loving appropriately and living with appropriate risk, spring up at the question. We invented them to let us approach that life. But they remind us of our own lives. They offer us a hope and a perspective, not of the past in which they were made—not that alone—but of the future. For if we lived in full response to the earth, to each other, and to ourselves, we would not breathe a supernatural climate; we would be more human.

The tendency of art and religion, and the tendency of poetic meaning, is toward the most human. It is a further humanity we are trying to achieve, at our most conscious, and to communicate.

The thinning-out of our response is the weakness that leads to mechanical aggression. It is the weakness turning us inward to devour our own humanity, and outward only to sell and kill nature and each other.

Trigant Burrow cautions us, in his essay "The Social Neurosis," not to "fall a prey to the common illusion that a disorder in social behavior is a disorder *outside* of man's own organism." The typical fallacy of normality, he believes, explains conflict "not as a condition of mind common to both contending parties, but as the 'wrongness' of the other fellow, the other group or the other nation." Hitler was able to announce his lies and offer them to us, like a bullfighter offering the cape. But we are not that furious beast of compulsive habit and compulsive thrust. We are a group of individuals; it was our own lies and wishes we were believing. Many of these lies had taken root then, and now they flourish.

How can a group of many people, bound in a balance of statehood, with its fundamental hope a tendency toward democracy, realize its full humanity? Has any group—any culture—ever done this?

We think of the Greek society, its lifetime, its limitations, and its effects, of the many contributive societies, known and little known, whose gifts and interpenetrations and conflicts reach our custom. What background is there for a criterion of imaginative maturity, in our society?

Our education molds us toward conduct, the outward and ethical are given lip-service, the outward and predatory are glorified by business society, and the young are brought up in conduct leading toward aggression surrounded by strict taboos. We know from the movies, the radio, and from every ad in the morning paper, what behavior is expected. We know what approvals are required from us; every day that knowledge is borne in on a flood of words.

Few enough among us who consider our society have spoken openly of the power to live. In his most plain and passionate book, John Collier writes:

"If the primitive group molded its members toward conduct

alone (which is tacitly assumed by most anthropologists as well as most laymen), then the group's significance to modern life would not be great. But if there is anything written clear across the almost infinite diversity of primitive society, it is that the group molds its members toward emotion, toward the experience of crises of realization and of conscience…. For the tribe to survive, even for the world to survive, requires intensity—intensity within form—in man. Hence, to a degree hardly imaginable in our modern society and state, the ultimate concentration of the primitive group is upon education—upon personality development. Every experience is used to that end, every specialized skill and expression is bent to that end. There results an integration of body–mind and of individual–group which is not automatic, not at the level of conformity and habit, but spontaneous, essentially spiritual, and at the level of freedom."

THE IMPOVERISHMENT OF IMAGINATION

In a group not molded toward such experience, we feel the penalties. We talk about these penalties in terms of mass and individual conflict; some call the process in which we find ourselves not its true name, but the death of culture; some call it the breakdown of moralities, the breakdown of communication.

We are cut off from large areas in ourselves, and we make the specialized skills and expressions our goals. We suffer from this, since the human process is only partly accomplished. We think in terms of property, weapons, secrets; we exalt the means. Less and less do our values have obligating power; less and less do we imagine ourselves and believe ourselves. We make a criterion of adjustment, which glorifies the status quo, and denies the dynamic character of our lives, denies time, possibility, and the human spirit.

This impoverishment of imagination affects our society, our culture, deeply.

THE DAMAGES TO THE AUDIENCE

Let us see in what ways the audience of poetry is injured by this waste.

Throughout our consideration of the imaginative and emotional response, I have used poetry as the index. As often as I do, I wish to remind you that it is used because it is a good index to our lives—and, yes of course, because it is here that I know the effects best. It is a good index *because* it is socially unacceptable. John Collier can see many things about our society precisely because he is looking at a relationship between it and the Indians, "ethnic groups of low prestige." But it is an index to our response, as a society, to many intensities.

What is the fear of poetry? To a great extent it is a fear produced by a mask, by the protective structure society builds around each conflict. The conflict, here, is a neurotic one, a false conflict based on a supposed antithesis of fact and relationship, of inner and outer effectiveness; it is a conflict upheld by the great part of organized society. The fear is a fear of disclosure, but, in this instance, of disclosure to oneself of areas within the individual, areas with which he is not trained to deal, and which will only bring him into hostile relationships with his complacent neighbor, whose approval he wants.

At this point he denies one of his most important functions and resources.

What must follow?

"Through the eclipse of large areas of the self," says Karen Horney in *Our Inner Conflicts*, "by repression and inhibition as well as by idealization and externalization, the individual loses sight of himself; he feels, if he does not actually become, like a shadow without weight and substance."

The individual is likely to think that he has actually become a richer personality during this amputation—it is really closer to an attrition of a major attribute. You have seen American men pride themselves on their aversion to art in general, feeling that this aversion gives them greater solidity, in fact greater reality. It is likely that the entire process is the attempt of a creature, stunted in one member, to become more whole by casting off the member. But this attribute, the poetic imagination, does not resemble the eye, which can be put out for its offense, so much as it resembles the blood, which must be strengthened by feeding.

The ensuing loss of energy can be seen in several of our group failures. The repressive codes that govern many of our media of communication—the Hays code (now under the Johnston office), which has acted like the distorting bottles of the *comprachicos* on the minds of most Hollywood writers, is one. And surely the movie producers, forming dwarfs and monsters as apparent as those made for the courts of Europe, are our modern *comprachicos*. The rules of commercial radio supply another such failure.

The breakdown in communication is an expression of this loss of energy. I shall return to this statement.

The loss, for the audience, is not a subtle or hardly perceptible reality. Its description has had, on the other hand, its greatest popular success when it has been most plain and detailed. The series of William Steig's drawings which have been appearing in books, in magazines (and in dance form), are incisive, ferocious, and not to be escaped. The faces of neurosis which they offer us, and which invariably evoke identification, are, as his brother points out in the preface to *All Embarrassed*, the faces of aversion of the American public to emotion—that neurotic coldness or embarrassment before disclosure, or intensity, which is one reason for so many jokes and so much tragedy in our lives.

Coldness of this sort accounts for a good deal of the response to poetry that says, "I have not the time," or "It bores me."

Contempt for other people accounts for as much; and is another result of the eclipse of an area in the personality. Publishers accept this contempt, which declares the imaginative level of the American audience to be that of a twelve-year-old, and keeps it there, by omitting the audience work that would make and acknowledge a change. Again, Hollywood works continually to keep its standard of contempt for the audience.

In his account of the broadcasts he made during the war over the public address system of a battleship to the men—the population of a city—below decks, John Mason Brown declares himself on this point. At the beginning of *To All Hands,* he writes:

"Some people, glancing through these pages before publication, have wondered why to so mixed a group, coming from such mixed backgrounds, I should have quoted, for example, from either Matthew Arnold or Shakespeare. There is only one rule for interesting people that I know of—and even it, alas, is not infallible—and this is to say to them as well as you can what interests you.

"Men may lack vocabularies, but men in danger share more thoughts than they are given credit for, because they share the same dilemma. Let death draw near and all men gathered together in twos or threes cease to be shy in their discussion either of it or of life. No school of philosophy can boast a better teacher than peril, when it approaches at a pace lively enough to be contemplated. As for Matthew Arnold and Shakespeare being read to men on their way into battle, there seems to me to be nothing strange or affected in this. The threatened beauties, the imperiled values, the free minds which they symbolize, supply this war with one of its most potent excuses.... The great poets are great for many reasons, among which is the simple fact that they are not fair weather friends....

"In my role,...it was my hope to amuse and my duty to try

to interest all these men. You cannot condescend to people you respect as much as I respect them."

The reader, the publisher, and the editor will all act out in their several ways impoverishment, with the occasional answers—from readers who have found poems which strike deep into their lives, from publishers who not from conscience but from their own wish print poetry, and from editors like John Mason Brown, who set human respect against the carping. The problem of the critic as audience—afflicted with the same impoverishment that all of us recognize—is a special one. This is not a book of literary criticism, and it will not deal with literary criticism. But the human problem of the critic seems to me a fascinating illustration of some of these issues. In our time, and along with the emergence of some criticism more penetrating and complete than any known to Western letters, we have seen our method come to dominance in the criticism of imaginative literature. We have seen the crooked ascendance of a sort of criticism by projection, in which the "critic" suffering from a specific form of guilt accuses the writer of that particular guilt. Now accusation is a classic form of criticism, guilt is common to this society and one of the pillar-themes of this literature. There would be nothing noteworthy in any of this. The curious identifying factor here is one common to all of this criticism by projection; it is the distinguishing trait of the method, and it marks it at once as neurotic. The accusation—which, as I said, may or may not be justifiable— is in every one of these attacks, supported by a lie. The reader is told that this is the proof of the accusation.* Now these details

★   The pattern is this: there is a general accusation, likely to be personal or political—it is hardly ever aesthetic—which is followed by an open lie. Then the accusation is declared proved. The only variation is that sometimes the accusation is not followed by a lie, but by two or more lies. Sometimes the lies are difficult to trace—if they are personal. More often, they are lies about the content of the work in question. A misreading will come in: the critic will accuse the poet of writing, say, about the American eagle in order to drag in a nationalist image, and when you look at the poem, you will see that there is a bird in it—as a matter of fact, two birds, one dead and one alive—but not eagles at all, alive, dead, or standardized. Or the lie may have no importance, except as unliterary—anti-literary—curiosities, and it probably is of no more importance that you see them so often under the names of critics who think of themselves as members of a group, a political group which appears to have no program but the attack of another group, and no direction except toward thinking of themselves as dangerous. They are not dangerous, of course. I know that if such people are "used" politically by a coherent and reactionary group they will be dangerous; of themselves, they are merely vicious, and the source of the viciousness is that same low level of energy which comes from impoverishment of the imagination.

The way to guard against their lies is the same as that prescribed by the fair practices groups in guarding against fraudulent salesmen: never agree to any statement you have not read thoroughly, and investigate all claims—they may be false.

THE "CORRUPTION OF CONSCIOUSNESS"

These forms of weakness—the ruling-out of emotion, overspecialization, aversion to the disclosure of oneself to oneself, the repressive codes, neurotic embarrassment and coldness, contempt for others, criticism by projection propped up with lies—are a cascade of penalties which cause suffering in those who feel them and in those on whom, in turn, their weakness is vented. They are all forms of what Collingwood names the corruption of consciousness.

follow a political generalization, after which the liar says (to prove his point)—"And my sister was involved with that poet," which the listening company knows to be a lie. Or the lies may follow a pattern now in use, I have been told, against writers. One of these attacks may supply the hostile opening: 1) The critic will say that the poet's most recent book is bad, but that the book before that was good, and the decline in the work is most unfortunate, and then produce the lie; 2) The critic will say that the poems all demonstrate one sorry fact about the poet (without, of course, offering the reader even a fragment for his consideration, and then produce the lie); 3) The critic will say that the poet is now engaged in some other activity (naming the means by which the poet earns a living), and was never really deeply in poetry anyhow, and then produce the lie. I happened to have learned that triad well, for the two critics who pointed out to me these approaches to lying went on to use them all.

"Consciousness," he says, "does not ignore a feeling; it disowns that feeling." Consciousness is defined as the "activity of thought without which we should have no terms between which intellect in its primary form could detect or construct relations. Thus consciousness is thought in its absolutely fundamental and original shape."

The statement, *This is how I feel*, implies a rejection of its opposite; and consciousness has "this in common with all forms of thought, that it lives by rejecting error. A true consciousness is the confession to ourselves of our feelings; a false consciousness disowns them."

The disowning is corruption: it is as if the consciousness permitted itself "to be bribed or corrupted in the discharge of its function, being distracted" toward an easier task. Imagination will share this corruption. It cannot do this if it is functioning positively. You cannot imagine falsely. The imagination is a function of belief and experience: that is, of course, why the realization of a poem is an event of belief and experience. This event takes place in a time-sequence involving the reverberation of images and sounds. The reaction is one in which discovery and memory are sealed together for you; and the relationship that seals them is what we call beautiful.

No, it is only in disowning that the falseness can reside; this is a country in which all activity is creative and true, and the only crime is treason, and the only treason is disowning.

Then the disowned element goes to work in your psychic life. Collingwood lists the corruptions of consciousness according to the psychologists' description, within the individual as repression, turned toward others as projection, massed in experience as dissociation, and in a selective structure (which is claimed) as fantasy. There is disaster in this habit; Spinoza taught this well, and Collingwood brings these meanings home again.

ARTIST, ARTWORK, AND AUDIENCE

In the artist, the problem of impoverishment of imagination arises also; for as art is common to both artists and audiences, consciousness is too, and the strengths and weaknesses of both are not particular to one category.

The one difference between the artist and the audience is that the artist has performed upon his experience that work of acknowledging, shaping, and offering which is the creative process. The audience, in receiving the work of art, acknowledges not only its form, but their own experience and the experience of the artist.

Both artist and audience create, and both do work on themselves in creating.

The audience, in fact, does work only on itself in creating; the artist makes himself and his picture, himself and his poem. The artwork is set to one side with a word, then, as we look at the common ground, the consciousness and imagination of artist and audience.

It may be said here in objection that the corruption of consciousness effects an impoverishment upon the artwork, and that there is good art and bad art. Of course there is an effect, a direct effect, for better or for worse. But I cannot acknowledge the way of thought that has given us so many double definitions of "good art" and "bad art."

A work of art is one through which the consciousness of the artist is able to give its emotions to anyone who is prepared to receive them. There is no such thing as bad art.

There is art and non-art; they are two universes (in the algebraic term) which are exclusive. We are considering art, its nature and the nature of its power for good; and we are fortunate in not having to be concerned with non-art.

It seems to me that to call an achieved work "good art" and an unachieved work "bad art" is like calling one color "good red" and another "bad red" when the second one is green.

And what about re-writing, you may ask, or correcting the line of a drawing? What about the work of the creative editor or critic? Improvement is sometimes conceivable, I would answer. It is possible to change a work of art in degree. But I doubt that it is possible to revise "bad art" into "good art" (and I renounce the terms). That would require not a change of degree but of kind, and it could not be done unless you changed the phase of the work, by as radical a process as changes water to steam: you would be making a new work.

A diagram of our statement might appear like this:

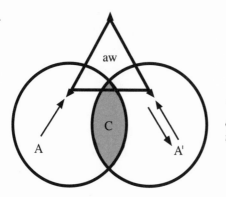

This diagram is false until all the components are shown in motion.

in which *A* is the artist, *A'* the audience, or witness, and *C* the consciousness of both, their common factor through which they communicate and share. In the diagram, *aw* is the artwork, seen in motion, and the vectors the relations to it.

These diagrams break down at once. Perhaps this one was made only to break down. For there is nothing exact here: these are not really vectors, they are arrows, since it is not possible to measure the amount of work of the audience. And there should be a small, almost invisible vector, I suppose, for the effect that the finished work of art has on the artist. Do you think it will influence his future work? Is not, rather, the work he did on it

influencing him? And what about the changes in both artist and
audience as a result of this experience—how are they to be shown?

THE DAMAGES TO THE ARTIST

The artist, in making himself, can be affected in several ways
by the general corruption of consciousness, the impoverishment of imagination which is at once a social and a deeply
folded-in subjective reality.

There is a general sneer, not so much at the individual poet,
as at the archetype. You will be able to trace its result in any poet
you know. You will see the defenses against it take countless
forms, ranging from the grotesque denial of its existence to a
mask to match its expectations, from a camouflage that allows a
city to regard the poet not as poet but as executive to the kind
of acceptance of the challenge that will send him out singing and
reading to the people or the acceptance which was one of the
motivations of this book.

A conspicuous form of impoverishment of imagination in the
artist—and I should like to confine the definition again to the
poet—is the denial of areas not only in himself but in his art. Here
he is reflecting society with a vengeance. The primary responsibility of the poet is to the human consciousness. But he does
respond; he responds to purity and to corruption. You may judge
how far corruption has gone when you reflect that most of our
poets accept it as a primary theme. Not only that: they tend to
absorb its methods, as we in war absorbed some of the methods
of the enemy. The poet stands in relation to Nature; this does not
mean landscape, as Robert Frost points out, but "the whole
Goddamn machinery." The machinery works according to the
laws of natural process; and the rule of perfection or death does
not hold in organic life. This is not a real choice, between an
absolute positive and an absolute negative, with only one moment

to choose. In a world of growth, the moment of choice may come as long as there is life. There is process: man can change and he can go on changing; at any moment he can do the work of re-creation on himself, and purify his consciousness.

The offer of perfection or death is one sign of impoverishment in the artist.

Another is the weakness that leads to judging the poem by its subject. During the war, how many poets despaired of writing of that suffering, as Owen or Rosenberg or Sassoon had in the war before? Some complained that there was nothing that did not illustrate the defeat of the individual by machinery. And now that the use of nuclear energy as a weapon has given us all the sense of peril of which John Mason Brown spoke, many poets speak in despair about the triumph of "the bomb" over life. Mr. Brown's meaning holds here, I believe; it seems to me that, sharing the sense of peril, we share more thoughts than we are given credit for; and that what appears as a feeling of separation is also the seed for a greater possibility of communication than ever in history.

The relation in all of this is made by sharing. Even the weak-nesses stem from the flaws in the wish to share.

The weakness of cliché, which is a product of corruption of consciousness and contempt for the audience: its mask is laziness.

The weakness of the "intentionally obscure" who have formed groups: these groups, you will discover, after the first few years of a fashion, are using the same expressions. Using the same words, not in the unique combinations of a style, but with the thinness of a sparse vocabulary that has set up a handful of images to denote the fantasy-life. But, in using these "obscure" terms, such writers have achieved their object, which was a double and conflicting object. One side of it was to shut themselves away from that part of the possible audience on whom they looked with contempt—and it is not hard to tell, from the poems, who were represented in this group; the other part of the object was to share experience and find an audience among those for whom they had no contempt. The first part included, of course, the show of that contempt. Now this is an ambition in conflict with itself, and it is that sense which dominates the writing of this type of poet. It is the poem in conflict *with itself* which is often produced, and which is so depressing to the reader.

The charge of obscurity, however, must be looked at very closely. It is one of the major charges brought against contemporary poetry, and it must always be taken as a declaration by the audience, which says "I find this poem obscure," and which tells us, at first, very much about the audience and nothing about the poem. It should rank with the complaint, "I do not understand this poem," as a statement descriptive only of the one who makes it. *Nothing has yet been said about the poem*, in either charge. If you are going to follow up this challenge, you must then inquire into the consciousness of the challenger. Is the challenger prepared to receive the poem? Or is this merely another way of disowning imaginative experience?

THE LANGUAGE OF DISTRESS

During illness, there is a breakdown in communication. Dr. Clyne Campbell has said that his insane patients showed one chief symptom: they were "unable to tell him clearly" what the matter was. That led him to conclude that "the language of distress might be part and parcel of the distress."

Surely the language is part of the state. But, if the patient cannot say what the matter is, he is not very different from others called well. Sometimes, also, the patient can tell suffering more acutely than one would guess, so that, as in reading this transcript of a four-year psychoanalysis finished at the Yale Institute of

Human Relations, one finds flashes which convert into insight the raw distorting pain. At one climax, the patient—a schizophrenic boy—says: "Just one thing...is there any psychological term at all that is the meaning of a person that just lives right in the present, a person that hasn't any ideas of his own, that is all ideas he's collected from other people, learned a great many things from books and from understanding and talking and experience, but he hasn't any of his own that he has figured out? Is that a certain type of person, or isn't it?" The analyst tells him that everyone does that to a certain extent, and the sick boy goes on, "That's the way I imagine myself."

A WAY OF GIVING: THE FULL-VALUED

There is another kind of poverty. It has nothing to do with any kind of "impoverishment." The other kind of poverty depends on a moment when everything is given. It is the human moment of equilibrium, and can hardly be separated from the renewal that is beginning. It comes in every profoundly human relationship; under this aspect, writing is only another way of giving—a courtesy, if you will, and a form of love.

But does one write in order to give?

One writes in order to feel: that is the fundamental mover.

The more clearly one writes, the more clearly will both the writer and the reader feel. But there must be imaginative truth—truth which is the health and strength and richness of imagination before poet or reader can approach the poem.

If that truth exists, it finds its form, for the truth of a poem is its form and its content, its music and its meaning are the same.

If that truth exists, and we are not locked away in defenses and denials, we move toward it, and it finds us.

Is there a risk of intensity, in this culture? Then, if we take that risk, the psychiatrists might declare we were adjusted to reality.

In another language, the word is not "adjusted" which implies a static condition to be adjusted to; the word is "full-valued," which accepts a world of process, a dynamic universe of time and growth relations.

The full-valued human being is capable of the total imaginative response. There is no threat to the self; the truth of the poem is taken.

PART TWO

BACKGROUNDS
AND SOURCES

CHAPTER FIVE

⊚

A CULTURE IN CONFLICT

American poetry has been part of a culture in conflict.

It is not the variety of our life, for that is easy to draw abundance from; I speak of the tearing that exists everywhere in Western culture. We are a people tending toward democracy at the level of hope; on another level, the economy of the nation, the empire of business within the republic, both include in their basic premise the concept of perpetual warfare. It is the history of the idea of war that is beneath our other histories. There we acknowledge the dynamic, and there many of our people see relationships tending toward equilibrium. In our periods of armistice, you hear everywhere, among the big-businessmen, the café owners, the untrained workmen, the unemployed, talk of another war—a next equilibrium toward which some efforts course, toward which all their inertia flows. This equilibrium is death. But around and under and above it is another reality; like desert-water kept from the surface and the seed, like the old desert-answer needing its channels, the blessing of much work before it arrives to act and make flower. This history is the history of possibility. Not vaguer than the other principle, it leads to definite things; but since these are future things, they cannot be described under the present daylight, the present poems are not their songs but will be their old ballads, anonymous, and their traditional tunes. All we can do is believe in the seed, living in that belief.

Indications are here.

Poetry has often failed us. It has, often, not been good enough. We want our poems; and there is little enough. But we know that what we need is to be made here, and that endurance has already found its concentration just here, in poetry that is denied and disowned and then in the storm remembered. During the London raids, newspapers in America carried full-page advertisements for *The Oxford Book of English Verse*, announced as "all that is imperishable of England." (Whitman's face was among the pictures; that concern is Oxford's.) The truth of that advertisement is there; it is as little possible to prove as many of the declarations I am making to you. There will be very little of what I say that will be possible for you or me to prove, or even to find tolerable examples; for the meanings are here, and they are proved by the logic of the imagination, and emotional laws, which not too many of our words have reached.

The immortality of these poems, then, is hardly in themselves, they go back to their earth which is the human spirit. Part of our labor will never be done; that is one kind of immortality. It is necessary that the twenty-fifth century know that we wrote trash. It is necessary that enough be done by then so that we all be seen resisting things which have for them changed and fallen away—transitional. Our poems will have failed if our readers are not brought by them beyond the poems.

Here is what Emerson said: "What we once admired as poetry has long since come to a sound of tin pans; and many of our later books we have outgrown. Perhaps Homer and Milton will be tin pans yet. Better not to be easily pleased. The poet should rejoice if he has taught us to despise his song; if he has so moved us as to lift us,—to open the eye of the intellect to see farther and better." That is Emerson, saying "tin pans"—but he does not speak with the voices we hear, talking about the "bad influence" of this poet and that social philosopher, talking in favor of agreements and schools, and against the experiments of the poet, who in our broken culture is still the most unofficial voice.

This country was begun in axiom-breaking. The church in New Haven is an image of its growth; for from the most violent denial came creation, the creative guilt made its new forms which hardened, so that the traditional building rested on the cornerstones of the murder of the king. There is a necessity, when an action has been taken which shocks the past life and must be justified, to set up another image as great as the murdered one, and stronger, and beyond the threats of killers. In the small instance, a church was set up. In the large instance, in our country which turned from the slaughter of Indians and the unremitting work of breaking land to the rationalism of Newton, Locke, and Montesquieu, it was the Constitution.

There were ideas of balance in the governments of his time which Newton felt, and political thought is bound to Newtonian science in the work of Newton himself. Politics, said Woodrow Wilson, is turned into mechanics under the touch of Montesquieu. The principle of unity depended, for each system, upon some single law. The law of gravitation swung the worlds, keeping the free bodies in their places, reined to their courses with order and precision. The poise and balance of forces gave the universe its unity, one of symmetry and perfect adjustment.

Wilson says, "The government of the United States was constructed upon the Whig theory of political dynamics, which was a sort of unconscious copy of the Newtonian theory of the universe." And, again, "The trouble with the theory is that government is not a machine, but a living thing. It falls, not under the theory of the universe, but under the theory of organic life."

Having described one fallacy, Wilson goes on toward another: he would hope that we would substitute the science of Darwin for the science of Newton.

BACKGROUNDS AND SOURCES

We cannot isolate the causal factors of a society and its culture without their relationships; and in our culture, with its demand for permanent patterns, we see a complicated danger, not caused by the flaws of any one method, but by the balance which has been attained, a balance of a perpetuated conflict, in which everything and every quality is set *against* another thing or another quality. Granted that the concept of good is at one pole and the concept of evil at another. Even they are not taken in their interplay. They have been shown as different in nature one from the other, and at that point art breaks down. Too much has been denied. In our art, when the fundamental principles have been achieved, so that the work of art can be seen as a system—a portion of the universe which we may separate in thought from all the rest in order to consider the changes occurring within it— we see that, in such a culture, it is not only good and evil, but evil as a problem and good as a problem, which we face.

I see the truths of conflict and power over the land, and the truths of possibility. I think of the concrete landscapes of airfields, where every line prolongs itself straight to the horizon, and the small cabin in the Appalachians under the steep trail streaming its water down; of the dam at Shasta, that deep cleft in the hills filled with white concrete, an inverted white peak with the blue lake of held water over it, and, over that, Shasta the holy mountain with its snows; New York at night when the city seems asleep and even asleep full of its storm and its songs; the house in the desert and the pool wooden-lidded against the sand, where poems are being read to the gold miners by the woman who came there to die of tuberculosis twenty-three years ago. I think of the lines of marchers before the fascist meeting, and the brown breasts of the policemen's horses, the feeling of being pushed back against the buildings of your streets; of the joyful dawn over the rivermouth, a boat riding down in slimness and white, and seeing three feet beyond the bow, a boy leaning like an angel on the air, for a moment there until I saw the harpooner's nest of the seagoing fisherman; of the hilltop in Birmingham, where from among the porticoes and classic pillars one can discern sudden flowing red and gold as far below the steel is poured; of the dark-paneled room high in the Empire State Building where all afternoon the heads of their companies said, the day of Stalingrad, "We will let the meanings go," and I think of the wretched houses of Gamoca where the Negroes lived and were brave, who are dead now of silicon in the lungs. And of the pride of the Embarcadero, recalling the general strike among the lights, the night the Bridge was opened—that marvelous red-painted bridge over our western gate; and of the eyes of the animals in the Sierra, gleaming along the roads; and of the people under the northern mountains; everywhere one learns forever that the most real is the most subtle, and that every moment may be the most real.

Of the crimes of those places: rape, arrogance killing the chance of life, the ignorant stoppage of youth, the poverty that invites every repressive force, the robbery of spirit, every kind of murder.

I think of the high sounds of wind in the stone walls of my city, and of the man who came to me, afraid that he would be murdered as he had charged the fascist with murdering. And the days of sunlight, when certain hopes were saved, and certain prisoners released, certain love realized.

In all this, richness, even to the most contradictory. I think of the monuments which combine and carry a blessing of purity, from the granite truncated wing of Kitty Hawk, with its stylized suggestion of feathers standing over the dunes and the ship-wrecked silver of that beach; around the base running the stainless steel and the Greek words about genius and about faith. From that wing to a little marker at Saratoga, nameless, with a boot covered by an epaulet in relief—the place where Benedict Arnold, who cannot be named, received the wound of the leg and won his crucial battle. And those places unmarked but dis-tinguishable, where Melville from the river each day ascended the ships he should have sailed; where Whitman walked the beach hearing in the surf and shore mixed songs, transparent songs of the mixing of life; where Hart Crane met the sea.

Many of our poems are such monuments. They offer the truths of outrage and the truths of possibility.

TO TEND TOWARD DEMOCRACY

Outrage and possibility are in all the poems we know, the long line from the first magic and the rituals of the heart and hero. Indeed, our poets are in their dread and music heroes of possi-bility as Shelley was, or of outrage as Rimbaud was, or of the process and relationship between the two—transformed by Dante into the soul's journey, and by Shakespeare annealed into every speech almost, almost into every breath.

In the early, Colonial poetry, not much is acknowledged of the conflicts spreading to the general scene. Freneau's "restless Indian queen" is queen of "a ruder race"—Edward Taylor makes the bread of life cry "Eat, eat me, soul, and thou shalt never die," with no particularization of individual consciousness; Anne Bradstreet takes up the endless dialogue of Western thought between the flesh and the spirit—the dialogue of separation which begets separation; Bryant glides over all, water-strider of that verse. Only with Emerson do we come to the "hope beyond hope," to Surface and Dream; and to the statement of the half-gods and the gods. Perhaps these conflicts are the old same war—I believe so—and truth or reality, process or moment, gods or half-gods, are the terms for immortal necessities, which are not checks and balances, but phases, if you will, of essence—all to be fought for, realized, and sung.

Surely they have their poets in our background. I do not think of Poe here, although in his disowning, in his selective fantasy, he spoke for something native to all of us—some appetite for life and permanence that could be threatened, partly by the conflict of the age, the machine-rigid cities, the brutal power which was an end in itself. So threatened, the appetite turns to violence and the grave—in Poe, in Fitz-James O'Brien, and much later, in our writers of violence and the romantic hunt of criminals.

MELVILLE AND THE PROBLEM OF EVIL

It is not until we reach, in our history, the poems of Melville—and I always except here the Indian chants, unknown to earlier times than this—that the conflict is open, and turned to music. All of Melville's prose announces the problem of evil—evil white-skinned and humped, one-legged and blasted, racing through the seas; or carried dumbly through ships and prisons and the hereditary tainted doom, or in the factories that are parables of woman's sexual life, or in the "spiritual inveteracies and malices" that enter every novel and every story. Innocence—Ishmael—is set with the others, and is sometimes saved.

But in the poems, the oppositions turn to music. The first draft of "Art" says:

> In him who would evoke—create,
> Contraries must meet and mate....

This is close to the center of the matter (as close as it is to Blake's "where opposites meet"). Simply, the line of culture was begun in America at a point of open conflict. All the wars of European thought began us, and Eastern balance has not yet come in. Melville knew both; his rejection of both was for the sea, and the future, perhaps. But it is outrage, the problem of evil, that is both on the surface, and deep, as in "Pebbles":

> *Implacable I, the old implacable Sea:*
> *Implacable most when most I smile serene—*
> *Pleased, not appeased, by myriad wrecks in me.*

The Civil War turned him into a poet who saw aspects of wars to come, veteran of a knowledge in some ways strange to his time, like the veterans in our own age of the war in Spain. "Now save thyself," he writes, "Who wouldst rebuild the world in bloom."

From the brilliant masked symbol in "The Portent" he draws the future and the war:

> *The cut is on the crown*
> *   (Lo, John Brown!)....*
> *Hidden in the cap*
> *   Is the anguish none can draw;*
> *So your future veils its face,*
> *   Shenandoah!*
> *But the streaming beard is shown*
> *(Weird John Brown),*
> *The meteor of the war.*

In the threats of the first winter, 1860–1861, he spoke clearly, writing "The Conflict of Convictions":

The People spread like a weedy grass,
  The thing they will they bring to pass,
And prosper to the apoplex.
The rout it herds around the heart,
  The ghost is yielded in the gloom;
Kings wag their heads—Now save thyself
  Who would rebuild the world in bloom.

He speaks of this conflict as "Tide-mark / And top of the ages' strife..." and leads into the refrain, a virile resolution:

The Ancient of Days forever is young,
  Forever the scheme of Nature thrives;
I know a wind in purpose strong—
  It spins against the way it drives....

YEA AND NAY—
EACH HATH HIS SAY;
BUT GOD HE KEEPS THE MIDDLE WAY.

In "Misgivings," the war has become "The tempest bursting from the waste of Time," and in "The March Into Virginia," written in 1861, Melville writes, "All wars are boyish, and are fought by boys."

It is not in the last two wars only that poets, among all the others, have spoken of the swallowing-up of the heroic warlike, the soldier-image, by machines. And surely this is an old complaint; it must go back to the shattering military invention, the invention of the stirrup, which made it so easy to hurl a spear from horseback. Stephen Spender said recently that poetry like Owen's, of the pity of war, was no longer possible. Melville was writing, in "A Utilitarian View of the Monitor's Fight," about a man in an ironclad—

> *War yet shall be, but warriors*
> *Are now but operatives; War's made*
> *Less grand than Peace,*
> *And a singe runs through lace and feather.*

He sets the recurrent seasons against death, even while he allows them memory, in "Malvern Hill"—

> *We elms of Malvern Hill*
> *Remember every thing;*
> *But sap the twig will fill:*
> *Wag the world how it will,*
> *Leaves must be green in Spring.*

He goes on with the open natural contradiction in

> *Gold in the mountain*
> *And gold in the glen,*
> *And greed in the heart,*
> *Heaven having no part,*
> *And unsatisfied men....*

Explicitly, in his lyrics, Melville sets up "Power dedicate, and hope grown wise," even though, as he says, in part in "The House-Top," and fully and succinctly in *Clarel*:

> *Ay, Democracy*
> *Lops, lops...*

The poet of the full consciousness, in prose and verse, he mourns; but his mourning is the true image-making work that is part analysis still. In "America," he describes:

So foul a dream upon so fair a face,
And the dreamer lying in that starry shroud.

This conflict penetrates. In the individual, it is sexual conflict; and, in any person, it can be seen in the search for a matching half of that human integral of two people; of whom any one is a fraction whose estimate comes through in the word "shied"— "And shied the fractions through life's gate"—

At the end of "After the Pleasure Party," with its overpowering sense of sexual threat, the prayer is to Urania, the "armed virgin," the "helmeted woman"—

O self-reliant, strong and free,
Thou in whom power and peace unite,
Transcender! raise me up to thee,
Raise me and arm me!

Before these lines the effort is described, for which the speaker is to be raised and armed: it is the longed-for remaking of self, or the setting free of the sexless component in order to pierce the mystery. The telling image works against itself, in a passage intended to be about sexlessness and at the same time to establish the selfhood of the *couple*. Here are the lines in full:

Could I remake me! or set free
This sexless bound in sex, then plunge
Deeper than Sappho, in a lunge
Piercing Pan's paramount mystery!
For, Nature, in no shallow surge
Against thee either sex may urge,
Why hast thou made us but in halves—
Co-relatives? This makes us slaves.

If these co-relatives never meet
Selfhood itself seems incomplete.
And such the dicing of blind fate
Few matching halves here meet and mate.
What Cosmic jest or Anarch blunder
The human integral clove asunder
And shied the fractions through life's gate?

Perhaps the clearing dealing with the parts of conflict are to be found in the short poem "Art," whose first draft was thrown away in favor of this:

Instinct and study; love and hate;
Audacity—reverence. These must mate,
And fuse with Jacob's mystic heart,
To wrestle with the angel—Art.

WHITMAN AND THE PROBLEM OF GOOD

It has been said, and there are lines in the poems to prove it, that Walt Whitman could not discriminate between good and evil, that indeed with his inclusive benevolence Whitman dismissed the problem of evil altogether. But it is not proved. As the critics add to their quotations, one thing comes through: Whitman from the beginning felt himself to be deeply evil and good. Within that conflict—again like the conflict of his culture—there was a *problem* of good. It was no matter of simple recognition, with direct action to follow. How was it possible to search for the good, find it, and use it? Whitman's answer was "Identify."

But, before Whitman could be, in his own words, likened and restored, he must deal completely with himself; and I think there has been no conflict deeper than the nature of that self ever solved in poetry.

Melville knew the sea, its poising and somnambulism, its levels of revery, the dive to blackness and the corposants, the memories of shore and sleep and love among disaster. Abstract among detail, he finds and finds; in his unresolved *Clarel*, his Pierre who acts and is doomed, and above all in *Moby-Dick* everything is essential, and more essential than it seems. But it is what it seems: the myth of tragedy rises up, world-shaped and enormous; Ahab is Ahab, and the Whale the Whale. If there is evil in whalehood; if there is evil in the chase; if darkness leaps from light; even so, there is redemption, and it lies in sympathy with another human being, in the arrival of a touch, and beyond that touch, of "the centre and circumference of all democracy," God our divine equality.

Whitman faced the same period and problem. His critics say that he does not discriminate between good and evil. F. O. Matthiessen in his full and powerful *American Renaissance*, declares of Whitman's "indiscriminate acceptance" that "it becomes real only when it is based on an awareness of the human issues involved, when it rises out of tenderness over man's struggle and suffering, and says, 'I moisten the roots of all that has grown.'"

This awareness of Whitman's is a process, lifelong, and whatever acceptance was finally reached expressed itself in an identification with America as a people, multitudinous and full of contradictions.

But, first, Whitman needed to accept himself. In the testimony of the poems, this most decisive step was the most difficult. Every trap was ready, just here. His idealized image was far from what he knew he was, in the late 1840's. Deeper than the acts of his living or the image-making of himself, his conflicts tore him: truth and reality were both at stake, and unless he could find them both, he would be lost to himself. His struggle was a struggle for identity.

He faced, not only good, but the *problem* of good.

Among his many faces, how was he to reach and insist on the good? How was he to be enough for himself, and take the terrible forms of earth also to be his own? How was he to identify, to talk of the expression of love for men and women, and see flashing that America—with its power, war, Congress, weapons, testimony, and endless gestation? America is what he identified with: not only the "you" in his lifelong singing of love and identification, but "me" also.

It was harder for Whitman to identify with himself than with the "you" of the poems.

To discover his nature as a poet and to make his nature by knowing it is the task before every poet. But to Walt Whitman, crowded with contradictions, the fifteen-year-old large as a man, the conventional verse-maker who learned his own rhythms at the sea-edge, the discovery of his nature was a continual crisis. He speaks of himself as ill-assorted, contradictory. His readers reacted violently from the beginning to his writing about sex— and of course it is not writing *about* sex, it is that physical rhythms are the base of every clear line, and that the avowals and the secrecy are both part of the life of a person who is, himself, a battleground of forces.

In the short conventional meter of "After the Pleasure Party," Melville's bitter pain at

The human integral clove asunder

makes its cry. Melville, however, was speaking of a couple—of himself as half, needing to mate with the "co-relative"—and crying out for the power to free sex by setting free the sexless essential man, or by remaking himself. Whitman, also, used these terms of need; but the "halves" he fought to bring together were in himself, and he chose, early in his life as a poet, not to allow himself the concept of a central sexless man, but to take the other way: to remake himself.

It is in the remaking of himself that Whitman speaks for the general conflict in our culture. For, in the poems, his discovery of himself is a discovery of America; he is able to give it to anyone who reaches his lines.

Apparent again and again are the relationships with himself, the people, and the "you" of any of the poems. From these relationships, we may derive the fact of his physical split with himself and the heroic quality of his struggle to achieve strength from that conflict. The report on his autopsy—performed necessarily with his consent, but actually at his request—speaks of the virtues as well as the decay of that body of a seventy-three-year-old man, the sound structures of his age, the diseases. The people who have read that report seem struck by nothing beside the statement of tuberculosis. Whitman had not complained of pain, and no diagnosis had been made in his lifetime. But there is another fact that leaps from the lines of the report. Long before any of the critical tests now being projected, little was known of glandular equilibrium. But the poems themselves speak for a struggle between elements in one man, and give us a resolution of components that are conventionally considered to be male and female—a resolution that expresses very much indeed. If you read, as I did, the report on the autopsy after the poems, you will find this deduction borne out by remarks which no writer— medical or lay—seems to have analyzed. The list—and this is a catalogue—includes one's specific expectation as a confirmation of many contradictory gestures, in his poems and his life. The statement is not emphasized, among the list of other tubercular areas and foci of infection, and one wishes simply to bring it to the attention of competent clinicians now. Here is declared, in the baldness of medical writing, that the left suprarenal capsule was tubercular, and contained a cyst the size of a pigeon's egg. The kidney was soft, red, swollen, somewhat granular. The smaller right kidney was in good condition.

Whitman's autopsy is used in Edgar Lee Masters' biography, but neither he nor anyone else has seemed to understand the implications of his finding. In the light of what we know about the suprarenal-pituitary-sex hormone relation, certain conclusions probably may be reached. I venture to suggest that the inclusive personality which Whitman created from his own conflict is heroic proof of a life in which apparent antagonisms have been reconciled and purified into art. If this is true, the definitions of good and evil, in relation to Whitman and his sense of possibility, may be re-explored.

The effort to make a balance must have been intense. When Whitman, in an early poem, speaks of the threat of being

lost to myself, ill-assorted, contradictory,

he shows us the beginning of a long and conscious work performed according to the challenges before a mythical hero. He wrote of the terrible doubt of appearances, and of himself among the shows of the day and night. He spoke of

the sense of what is real, the thought if after all it should prove unreal....

This struggle was not a struggle for conformity in the "normal," but for the most intense reality which the individual can achieve, a struggle of process and hope and possibility which we all make when we desire to include our farthest range and then extend the newly created self into the new again, when we base our desire in the belief that the most real is the most subtle, in art and in life.

It was Whitman's acceptance of his entire nature that made the work possible. The line of a man full of doubt is

I never doubt whether that is really me....

Will went into this work on the self, and there are signs of the achievements here as well as the scars. Whitman is accused by many of showing too much will, and we know how unlikely it is for the efforts of will alone to lead to form. The form of Whitman does not arrive as a product of will, line by line. Each poem follows the curves of its own life in passion; it stands or falls, dies or grows, by that. The form is there, but it is a form of details. For the large work is a double work, and we must seek form in its two expressions: the entire collection of *Leaves of Grass,* and the life-image of Whitman as he made himself, able to identify at last with both the people in their contradictions and himself in his. Able to identify—and this is his inner achieve-ment—with his own spirit, of which his body, his life, his poems are the language.

For Whitman grew to be able to say, out of his own fears,

Be not afraid of my body,

and, out of his own scattering,

I am a dance.

He remembered his body as other poets of his time remem-bered English verse. Out of his own body, and its relation to itself and the sea, he drew his basic rhythms. They are not the rhythms, as has been asserted, of work and lovemaking, but rather of the relation of our breathing to our heartbeat, and these measured against an ideal of water at the shore, not beginning nor ending, but endlessly drawing in, making forever its forms of massing and falling among the breakers, seething in the white recessions of its surf, never finishing, always making a meeting-place.

Not out of English prosody but the fluids of organism, not so much from the feet and the footbeat except as they too derive from the rhythms of pulse and lung, Whitman made his music signify. Rarely, in the sweep of lines, is the breath harshened and interrupted. The tension of Hopkins is nearer to activity: it is activity, muscular, violent, and formal. Emily Dickinson's strictness, sometimes almost a slang of strictness, speaks with an intellectually active, stimulated quick music. But Whitman offers us the rhythms of resolved physical conflict. When he says, "I have found the law of my own poems," he celebrates that victory.

Forced by his own time to see the industrial war, the war of the States, the disavowal of death (one of the deepest sources, in our culture, of the corruption of consciousness), Whitman's fight for reconciliation was of profound value as a symbol. The fight was the essential process of democracy: to remake and acknowledge the relationships, to find the truth and power in diversity, among antagonists; and a poet of that democracy would have to acknowledge and make that truth emerge from the widest humanity in himself, among the horizons of his contradicted days and nights. The reconciliation was not a passive one; the unity was not an identification in which the range was lost (although "Identify" is a key word in his work); the peace toward which his poems tended was not simply a lack of war. He put away the war he had known, in the hospitals, as a pioneer in what is now called psychiatric nursing. He did that as he put away, in writing a dirge for Lincoln, the fact of the murder. It was simply that, to Whitman, the life, the fact of Lincoln's death, and the "debris and debris of all the slain soldiers of the war" were more immediate in this "death's outlet song." In a minor poem of four lines, he uses one line to call the assassination

> *...the foulest crime in history known in any land or age,*

and we can see that the line is thrown away. It is a "bad line," and with it Booth is dismissed. So, this poet will say, of slavery,

> *On and on to the grapple with it—Assassin! then your*
> *life or ours be at stake, and respite no more.*

These are flat lines, the power of music is lost. On these, and on the "catalogues," charges are made that Whitman is full of "bad lines," and that he is a "bad influence."

Whitman is a "bad influence"; that is, he cannot be imitated. He can, in hilarious or very dull burlesques, be parodied; but anyone who has come under his rhythms to the extent of trying to use them knows how great a folly is there. He cannot be extended; it is as if his own curse on "poems distill'd from poems" were still effective (as it forever is); but what is always possible is to go deeper into one's own sources, the body and the ancient religious poetry, and go on with the work he began.

As for the "cataloguing" lines: it seems to me that they stand in a very clear light, not only among his poems entire, but also in regard to present techniques.

There has been a good deal of regret over the printed poem, since first the press was used; and recently, with the mourning over a supposed breakdown in communication, I have heard simple people and college presidents complain that the function of the poet is past, that the bard is gone. Now it is true that a poem heard does enter very vividly into the consciousness; but, with the habit of reading as widespread as it now is, many prefer to see the poem, at least to see it before hearing it, and this is apart from that number who can imagine better when they read than when they listen. For those who care more for the hearing of poetry, there is the stage and the radio, mediums allowing very little verse to make itself heard, except in such ways as I propose later to show. But, whether a poem is approached through the eyes in a book, or through the ears, the eyes within the eyes, the visual imagination, are reached; and this in itself is a way of reaching the total imagination. This visual summoning may be made often or very seldom, depending on your poet; if the occurrence is well prepared, the impact is unforgettably strong. The visual imagination may be spoken of as including the eyes. The imaginative function includes the senses. It includes, perhaps most easily, a kind of seeing; we are perhaps most used to having sight invoked in the telling of stories and poems.

Whitman draws on this continually, sometimes with a word at a time—

> *The birth, the hasting after the physician, the beggar's tramp,*
> *the drunkard's stagger, the laughing party of mechanics,*
> *The escaped youth, the rich person's carriage, the fop, the eloping*
> *couple,*
> *The early market-man, the hearse, the moving of furniture into*
> *the town, the return back from the town,*
> *They pass, I also pass—*

Sometimes these visual summonings are accomplished in a procession of short phrases:

> *Passage to more than India!*
> *O secret of the earth and sky!*
> *Of you O waters of the sea! O winding creeks and rivers!*

Of you O woods and fields! of you strong mountains of
    my land!
Of you O prairies! of you gray rocks!
O morning red! O clouds! O rain and snows!
O day and night, passage to you!

Sometimes they follow each other line after line:

With the fresh sweet herbage under foot, and the pale
    green leaves of the trees prolific,
In the distance the flowing glaze, the breast of the river,
    with a wind-dapple here and there,
With ranging hills on the banks, with many a line
    against the sky, and shadows,
And the city at hand with dwellings so dense, and stacks
    of chimneys,
And all the scenes of life and the workshops, and the
    workmen homeward returning.

These successions are not to be called catalogues. That name
has thrown readers off; it is misleading. What we are confronted
with here, each time, is not a list, but a sequence with its own
direction. It is visual; it is close to another form, and its purpose
is the same as the purpose which drives this passage:

And Sutter, on his way home—
—passes through the prosperous landscapes of a happy
    countryside.
Wealth, fertility and contentment can be sensed
    everywhere.
The rain has ceased.... Myriads of raindrops shimmer
    in the sunshine.

> *Suddenly, he meets a group of working people with*
> *picks, and pans for gold-washing.*
> *Astonished, Sutter follows them with his eyes, then turns*
> *his horse and gallops towards the fort.*
> *The store-keeper from near the fort comes up to Sutter to*
> *show him gold dust in the palm of his hand.*
> *He asks Sutter if this is really gold or not.*
> *Sutter nods slowly.*

That sequence describes a key action; in the next few lines,

> *The dams are taut with their heavy loads, the canal locks*
> *are shattered, and the waters rush through their old*
> *courses.*

You will recognize the form of that passage, if you imagine it with your eyes. It is typical, and it is very like Whitman. But it is a fragment of the script of a movie called *Sutter's Gold.*

Whitman, writing years before the invention of the moving picture camera, has in his poems given to us sequence after sequence that might be the detailed instructions, not to the director and cameramen only, but to the film editor as well. The rhythm of these sequences is film rhythm, the form is montage; and movies could easily be made of these poems, in which the lines in the longer, more sustained speech rhythms would serve as sound track, while these seemingly broken and choppy descriptive lines would serve well as image track.

THE POETS OF OUTRAGE AND THE POETS OF POSSIBILITY

But the chief reason for the difficulty that certain critics and imitators have with Whitman is not in his rhythm nor his "lists." These can be translated; we can see in our own time that a powerful poet can take his long, breathing line and transform it to his own uses and his own music. What has to be changed radically is the meaning. In Jeffers' hands, the long line of Whitman—which does, of course, lead us to Biblical and to Greek poetry—has been transformed. The meaning has crossed over, and is with the antagonists in our long conflict, both sides of which we know so well, from both sides of which the various and beautiful strength does arrive. Jeffers in his power has set the alternative of perfection or death. Wanting perfect love, perfect human beings, perfect acts, he sees death as the only other truth. In an organic world, if you set that choice, death is the answer; if you do not see a perfection of its own kind and moment, moving in time through many things, there is no other answer but annihilation. The setting of this alternative is a product of an age of mechanistic science, which could let its people speak of each other in terms of inorganic structure, which saw the universe infinitely large, and dying.

Whitman is the emblem poet, in this conflict, of another relationship. He is the poet of possibility. And he gives the meanings of possibility, produced by his own age, their further meaning and image in poetry.

Melville is the poet of outrage of his century in America, Whitman is the poet of possibility; one cannot be repeated more than the other. But Whitman's significance is based on the possibility realized in his period, as Dante's is based on the system of his religion in his time. As far as their imagination of *possibility* outranges their time, their systems live; for their images are deep in their belief. Melville's outrage lives; he touched perpetual evil, the perpetual hunt, and sea-images, world-images gave these their language. They speak for the backgrounds of our present. In our history, our open history, we know the gifts of many poets: in our buried history are the lost poems and songs; but these two master-poets, in all their work, stand at the doors of conflict, offering both courage and possibility, and choosing, emphasizing one or the other according to the ways in which forces that work in all of us drove them, and were driven, as they lived toward their forms.

CHAPTER SIX

CHOICE AND THE PAST

There is also, in any history, the buried, the wasted, and the lost.

In the life of this people, we have seen some of that sub-merged continent of song surface and take its place. But in this society, perhaps more than in any other, because of all the arrivals which brought its people to it, determined to live differently from before, there is and has been a great submergence. In many families, we were parented by the wish to move differently, to believe differently—that is, more intensely—from the past and the past place. Many came freely, inviting all the risk. I think of those others—stolen from beside African rivers, seduced by promises of land and work, who reached harbor and found the homestead underwater, the work a job of conscription; and those in Mexico who were promised an American education, and arrived to find themselves signed to four years at the hottest place in the assembly line; and those newly come from the camps of Europe who wake in the Louisiana swamp. Their awakening is sharp, and we can tell their dreams. They do not long for home; they long for America. What of the others—born to mine-towns and the cave-in under the house floor, driving the night trucks packed with high explosives, anonymous in the schoolrooms, the outcast teacher among the very young? Their songs have been lost as the songs of the unborn. Or the happy, who kiss lying in the park—who dive in the clear branchwater and rise dripping to April in the South and sing their lost songs among the green of our seasons as well as among our freezing rigid power? Dead power is everywhere among us—in the forest, chopping down the songs; at night in the industrial landscape, wasting and stiffening the new life; in the street of the city, throwing away the day. We wanted something different for our people: not to find ourselves an old, reactionary republic, full of ghost-fears, the fears of death and the fears of birth. We want something else.

We see the symptoms and the symbols of the conflicting wishes in our poetry.

They are among us, the voices of the present, the famous voices and the unacknowledged, and the voices of the past. We may choose; we are free to choose, in the past as well as now, and there is a tradition at our hand.

THE BURIED HISTORY: SOME RITUAL CHANTS

Behind the past of any of us is that moment of arrival, with its song.

The tribes do not have that: their creation myths are based on this continent. In their relation to our culture, which had denied them and starved them at the root, they tell us that they still live, and that we may rise to full life at any time. Collier speaks of the Indian excellences, even as an "ethnic group of low prestige." In "critical action" they excel; the war proved them. "In rhythm, so little regarded in our white society, the Indians excel. In public spirit they excel, and in joy of life, and in intensity realized within quietude. They excel in art propensities, and in truthfulness."

The buried voices of the Indian chants have hardly reached our written literature. Rafinesque, Mary Austin, John Neihardt, have translated some ceremonial poetry; a few others have forced Indian images on poems of their own, with as choppy and unabsorbed a set of results as we have seen, during the last few years, in those poets who have used Lorca, whole and unassimilated, corrupting the fiery purities of his Spanish into a grotesque of English.

A few songs carry over. In recording Hastiin Klah's singing of the Navajo Songs, Dr. Harry Hoijer translates the "There Are No People" song with its refrain,

You say there were no people: smoke was spreading over (the earth);
You say there were no people: smoke was spreading over (the earth);

and the "Song of the Flood," which begins,

They are running from the water; I came up with it;
When my spiritual power was strong; I came up with it;
When it was holy; I came up with it.

and the song "When They Saw Each Other," here in full:

The first man has it in his hands; he has the sun in his hands;
In the center of the sky, he has it in his hands;
As he holds it in his hands, it starts upwards.

The first woman has it in her hands;
She has the moon in her hands;
In the center of the sky, she has it in her hands;
As she holds it in her hands, it starts upwards.

The first man has it in his hands;
He has the sun in his hands;
In the center of the sky, he has it in his hands;
As he holds it in his hands, it starts downwards.

The first woman has it in her hands;
She has the moon in her hands;
In the center of the sky, she has it in her hands;
As she holds it in her hands, it starts downwards.

These are the dance rhythms brought into poetry; the footbeat is heard, even through translation; the repetition gives us at once the ritual and bare strength.

In the Indian culture, the songs had religious presence. We have the spectacle of a culture that values its poetry driven into captivity and repression by a power-culture that sets no store on this art.

THE PROMISE OF FUNCTION

How can we see art in America freed from the power which denies it?

One art will let us see the ways in which an accepted group may move ahead. Architecture, locked as it is to our economy, has made a history in which are implicit the histories of the unaccepted. In building, our second largest production field, the involvements and requirements of the people are answered or disowned. The results are easy to see, in spite of their far-reaching complications: in fire reports; in police records of robbery, incest, promiscuity; in the social workers' casebooks, as well as in the skyline where pride runs along with our following eyes. The relation between men and buildings has been told in James Marston Fitch's clear, condensed *American Building*. He repeats Horatio Greenough's definitions, saying, "Like Walt Whitman, but with more precision, he saw in the burgeoning American industry the material basis for a new esthetic standard, one which would be in conformity with advancing science and technology instead of increasingly in opposition to it. Here his

confidence in the creative genius of the plain people was not viti-
ated, as was Ruskin's, by a Tory's fear of giving them too much
freedom. It was they who would fashion the new American
beauty—not the intelligentsia nor the artists nor the wealthy and
well-bred connoisseurs....

"What kind of beauty could we expect of them? Greenough
answered with poetic and electrifying precision: 'By beauty I
mean the promise of function. By action I mean the presence of
function. By character I mean the record of function....'

"When Greenough spoke,...he voiced the aspirations of the
most progressive section of mid-century American democracy.
It is this reality—democracy, science, industry—which he
accepts as the essential basis for effective esthetic standards. This
reality is the source of his buoyant confidence, enabling him to
envisage a democracy so complete as to render esthetic falsehood
impossible. His buildings would have no ulterior esthetic
motive—no intangible job of intimidation, repression, or
deceit—precisely because the society of which they were a part
would have no such motives."

Now these statements stand forth plain and clear as any building, a dense and realized structure. That conviction is part of an
art which is being used and is thoroughly conscious of it—as
used and conscious as the Indian songs are on their level.

CERTAIN MISFORTUNES

But, alongside, we know that even with the conviction in
Whitman, he set up and printed *Leaves of Grass* himself, and said
that he gave away more copies than he sold. The best-selling
book of verse of those years was a book called *Fern Leaves From
Fanny's Portfolio. Moby-Dick* had bad reviews; most of the copies
were burned in the fire at the Harper warehouses. Percival, the
most popular poet before Bryant, a poet who made the first

attempt in our history to write the meeting-place between the kind of experience which may be called scientific, and poetry, is ignored. More than ignored: he is referred to in all the anthologies as a one-poem poet, and then a poor imitative poem, "The Coral Grove," is printed. Emily Dickinson, whose unappeasable thirst for fame was itself unknown for years after her death, had to fight through her family—"Vesuvius at home"—until a miserable lawsuit and the theft of a manure pile interrupted the posthumous publication of her work, and postponed for forty-nine years what may be her finest book. Hart Crane was bitterly attacked; one of our critics called him insane; and the Greenberg manuscript, a most rich source to him, did not appear for many seasons after its own poet's tragic death.

And what of the songs?

THE LOST, THE ANONYMOUS, THE DREAM-SINGERS

On work gangs, prison gangs, in the nightclubs, on the ships and docks, our songs arise. From the Negroes of this country issue a wealth of poetry, buried in that it never touches its full audience; it touches few poets; but it passes, as song, into the common air at once, stirring forever those who hear blues and shouts, the dark poetry.

The continent in its voices is full of song; it is not to be heard easily, it must be listened for; among its shapes and weathers, the country is singing, among the lives of its people, its industries, its wild flamboyant ventures, its waste, its buried search. The passion is sung, beneath the flatness and the wild sexual fevers, contorted gothic of the Middle West; the passion is sung, under the regret and violence and fiery flowers of the South; the passion is sung, under the size and range and golden bareness of the Western Coast, and the split acute seasons of the cities standing east.

Children sing their games, work gangs their hammer-measures:

meaningless rhymes, some say, but it is not so. The meaning is here; it is the game of the work, their rhythms set by songs. And in the hospitals, poems arrive, and in the quiet rooms at home; the little book in the hand, the long perceptive gaze; in the TB ward, at lunch hour in the shop, in the bunkhouse of the lumber camp, and in the extremity of the mental institution, the poems rise; and on the battlefield, lost and forgotten, as truth is found—sharp emotional truth in a flash of life—the poems rise.

One may speculate about the lost poems. The folklore scholars, the anthropologists, have found many of them again; the teachers of children, men like Hughes Mearns, have discovered and instigated many, and kept us from their loss; poets and editors like Louis Untermeyer have again and again taken up the first work of new poets, as he privately printed the first book of Stephen Spender; the little magazines, for a while flourishing (so that Cecil Day Lewis could say to me, "There is a place for poetry in America as long as the little magazines survive—"), could save many more. However, what of the dream-singing and its songs? I think of California in 1870, when the Indian tribes, after their final subjugation, turned to dream-singing, sang their hope that the ghosts of their fighters would come back riding, to fight again and this time have the victory. Then, in the next season, they lost that hope, and dreamed—like the Europeans in the camps— singing of how they themselves would save themselves, and would rise and fight; and then, losing that promise, began to tell, to sing their dreams, fusing their wishful dreaming.

Belief has its structures, and its symbols change. Its tradition changes. All the relationships within these forms are interdependent. We look at the symbols, we hope to read them, we hope for sharing and communication. Sometimes it is there at once, we find it before the words arrive, as in the gesture of John Brown, or the communication of a great actor-dancer, whose gesture and attitude will tell us before his speech adds meaning from another source. Sometimes it rises in us sleeping, evoked by the images of dream, recognized in the blood. The buried voices carry a ground music; they have indeed lived the life of our people. In times of perversity and stress and sundering, it may be a life inverted, the poet who leaps from the ship into the sea; on the level of open belief, it will be the life of the tribe. In sub-jugated peoples, the poet emerges as prophet.

"The artist must prophesy," writes Collingwood, "not in the sense that he foretells things to come, but in the sense that he tells his audience, at risk of their displeasure, the secrets of their own hearts."

The dreaming Indians, then, in the spring of the next year, found they were dreaming in patterns. This, the most private, the most "obscure" of makings, was shared; they were dreaming the same dreams.

Acknowledging that, the core of prophecy in loss and exile, they made their new religion. They began to sing their dreams.

JAMES GATES PERCIVAL

James Gates Percival is, in many ways, the lost poet of meeting-places. Poet, philologist, physician, geologist, New England eccentric, he combined the "fields" of thought in a way that has been outlawed since Descartes. He translated Malte-Brun's geography; he went to Charleston to practice medicine, but soon closed his office, saying, "When a person is really ill, he will not send for a poet to cure him." In 1822, he was asked to read the Phi Beta Kappa poem in New Haven; but when he faced the meeting, with his "Prometheus," he suddenly knew he could not. Percival, the tall, shabby, thin man, who was known to live on crackers and dried beef, the mad rock-smasher who walked around town in his sheepskin cap and gray cloak, confessed that he was discouraged with the poem, and sat down in disgrace.

The poem he would not read begins in a jumble of influences, and suddenly, after the tenth stanza, breaks into light:

> *The whole machine of worlds before his eye*
> *Unfolded as a map, he glances through*
> *Systems in moments, sees the comet fly*
> *In its clear orbit through the fields of blue,*
> *And every instant gives him something new,*
> *Whereon his ever quenchless thirst he feeds;*
> *From star to insect, sun to falling dew,*
> *From atom to the immortal mind, he speeds,*
> *And in the glow of thought the boundless volume reads.*
>
> *Truth stands before him in a full, clear blaze*
> *An intellectual sunbeam....*

The poem goes ahead in praise of possible mastery, remembering the spring of the world and the newborn ancients who leapt mind's barriers—

> *The times are altered:—man is now no more*
> *The being of his capabilities;...*

He asks for men who can feel the beauty of simplicity and deal their blows. He praises Rome, just freed, calling for a new world in the year of liberty. Here are the mighty months; but, in revulsion from Europe, he speaks of Freedom and against the endless blood and tyrants of the older countries. Dealing with the material of Shelley, he goes ahead with the scientific consideration of mind:

> *...designed*
> *As the one balance, which at least can stay*
> *Awhile the haste of causes...*

The spirit, he cries, has energies untamed by all its fatal wan-
derings. On the journeys of the spirits,

> *Space is to them an ocean, where they rush*
> *Voyaging in an endless circle; light*
> *Comes from within....*

His poetry was outcast. That is, the most trite, hackneyed, imitative passages were praised by Whittier, who said that the rest
was "wrought up in defiance, it would almost seem, of the natural laws of association and the common rules of composition";
and Lowell tried to demolish Percival in a wildly destructive piece
of criticism. The word of these powerful critics was accepted.
Percival is remembered for

> *Deep in the wave is a coral grove*
> *Where the purple mullet and gold-fish rove,*

and the rest, the "vast theme" on which trembled his heart, is
lost and forgotten, although the books exist.

SECRECY AND THE GIBBS PAPERS

When the books do not exist, we must visit the houses for the
papers themselves. In *Ancestors' Brocades* and the preface to *Bolts
of Melody*, Millicent Todd Bingham tells of the camphor-wood
chest, and of the little tune the lock plays as you turn the key.
In 1929, Mrs. Bingham heard that tune as she opened the chest;
she saw what had been lying in the long darkness, poems including the one beginning:

The things that never can come back are several—
Childhood, some forms of hope, the dead;
But joys, like men, may sometimes make a journey
And still abide....

The reader stands at that lock; and the rights of the reader are not determined. What of Lady Byron burning the letters? What of Max Brod, breaking his promise to Kafka? And these poems of Emily Dickinson's? How much shall we leave to natural waste here? How much of the loss is the story of our art, with its curious penalties and guilts under this cultural sun?

I know the story best through work I have done on the papers of Willard Gibbs. Denied access to the material, insulted as a writer, attacked as the book appeared, my ancestry vilified, I know some of the effects of that hostility and rage which was, to me, deeply a part of Gibbs' own story, part of the causes of the buried life of which I speak. But it took interesting forms: the family tried to stop publication of the book by browbeating its publisher, and did stop certain publication abroad; E. B. Wilson, a student of Gibbs' and a man who should have written his life and had, in fact, given up the work several times, printed a statement saying that, since he did not recognize the portrait of Gibbs—an early photograph in the collection at Yale—it could not possibly be Gibbs. Later he wrote to a scientist who had worked with him to say that he, Wilson, had looked into my origins, and that for me to be writing about Gibbs, my ancestry being what it is, was as bad as for a Negro to be writing about a Southern gentleman. At the same time, the libraries at Yale and at Johns Hopkins and Harvard, and the New York Public Library, were full of their customary generosities. Only once was a remark made that offered a hint about this kind of burial. Only once did a librarian assure me that the Gibbs material I was using would not be shown again until my book appeared. My work did not, of course, depend on privacy of information; I was able to show her that. But the attitude, assuming that ideas are property, setting up monopolies on imaginative work, were apparent everywhere in this story. I came to understand the manifestations as part of Gibbs' afterlife and life.

CONCEALMENT AND THE ARTIST

There is a concealment that is of a different nature. It may take various forms; it always has to do, I think, with a special concern for the majority. I remember a meeting with André Breton after I had translated an introduction of his to a book of "primitive" paintings. We spoke of publishing. "I would never publish anywhere," he said, "unless I knew that there I and my followers constituted a majority." (See Chapter Four, The Damages to the Artist. This attitude, certainly, stands in direct relation to the forming of groups of the "intentionally obscure.")

A more attractive attitude of defense was disclosed at a café. In one corner, a man was playing a guitar, and the stranger turned to watch him. The guitar player was good; the stop and tremble of the strings touched everyone in that room. "You know," said the stranger, "I respect creative people, any kind; I never used to feel that way, but something happened—I know a man in the city I come from, a business associate (I'm a lawyer)—we've gone on fishing trips for twenty years—I know him fairly well, I'd say—big man, too: six foot four, weighs two hundred and forty pounds. Twenty years, and I just found out last month that he writes poems. I asked around; he's written books of them; very good, too, they say. I'm going to get ahold of some. But I sure feel different about creative people."

"What is the name of your friend?"

"Wallace Stevens," said the stranger.

These are both stories in the relationship toward the majority, toward the reader and the potential reader; and toward the
unknown. "Whom do you write for?" Gertrude Stein was
asked. "Myself and strangers," she answered.

Where is the stranger, the reader, in the half-light of the
buried life?

THE SINGING BONES

The rights of the reader are, surely, the rights of the people.
What are these rights in reference to art? If works of art, the
Dickinson manuscripts for example, were placed in the public
domain, it has been explained to me, there would be an end of
the profits of their publishing; if the implications were to be followed, there'd be the end of "the art business."

Some poetry is in the public domain from birth. John Henry
and Stormalong sprang wellborn in song before us; they belonged
to us all, the Olympian company, before they belonged to anyone, except in the forgotten moment of conception. I do not
speak now of the many songs we do not know: miners' songs of
the past, the songs of the Chinese workmen on the western rail-
ways, the poems of the Nisei camps, the lost songs of the slave
underground. But of folksongs of heroes, and the chanteys and
cowboy songs, the haunting ranch ballads that rise again as popular songs about Laredo, about the ghost-herd—of "Shenandoah"
as it is sung, the curtain rising on a stage of O'Neill's; of the
Shaker songs appearing again in Copland's music, and the hymns
and marches in Ives'; of the calypsos and their tabloid ballads syn-
copated in rhythms which were hardly here before they were in
every jukebox; of the strike songs. Of "Joe Hill." Of the generation's folksingers who move between the libraries and the
broadcasting studios. And of the poets who have reached back to
these sources for their inner myths: published and unpublished,

from Sandburg to the new manuscript just come to my desk.

And of Bessie Smith, that woman of the songs, whose body made music, whose death in blood and denial hangs over our singers, whose blues are beginning now to be printed, although they have never stopped being sung.

Of the reading of lost poems in the meeting halls and the union halls and in the quiet rooms of friends.

And of the legends, especially a legend common to many lands, told here as of a father with countless children, never missing any as he ate his meat night after night, until darkly he began to dread and wonder. Yes, they were dead, they were murdered by his wife. He found their bones, singing on the heap, and then he knew.

That is the legend of our buried poetry.
The dead children and the singing bones.

PART THREE

THE "USES"
OF POETRY

CHAPTER   SEVEN

@

THE ARTS OF AMUSEMENT: A DANCE SEQUENCE

Never in our history have our popular arts offered more full or wide-ranging gifts; never have they been more direct in their vitality, more native in their assertion. Almost all levels are represented in our enjoyments: from the nightclub to the evening radio, from the on-the-spot newscast to the jam session, the feature film and the animated cartoon, the game as seen and the game as reported, television theater and musical comedy—the sparkle and attraction of all of them are at a peak of technical achievement. The approval that they make in the audience is happy and overpowering at those moments of superlative grace that call for complete enjoyment and agreement. The typical climax is that of the modern musical-comedy dance: I think of Gene Kelly dancing with his "other self" in a Technicolor movie. The dance is a brilliant hybrid of tap and ballet. More completely than any outside exposition could do, the hero acts out his despair, his self-contempt, his eternal lightness and the effectiveness of his hope, that will indeed bring him his love and his perfection: in a shattering gesture (translated from Cocteau's image), he leaps through a storefront window and achieves his unity.

The audience, in such moments, is expressed. The solving of

emotion through dance, in which the dancer becomes the solution, in which gaiety and skill make their accord and triumph,
and the romantic hero and the hypnotic *Doppelgänger* also make
their accord—the pleasure of the watcher is a ripple across the
emotions, a ripple across the muscles, and evidence of a high level
in easy moments among those arts which are *not* as poetry is to
us. These are the amusement arts, and they differ from art
because they are a means to an end. The effect is calculated and
the audience is calculated.

It is possible to say, about this dance, that thus we distract ourselves from our conflict, which reaches us tapped out in
contrapuntal rhythms; to say, about the hero, that his conflict was
meaningless, and left him where he had always been, would
always be; and about the heroine that she who was intended to
stylize for the public—lined in rows and sitting in the dark—to
stylize love and sex, was neither, but again and again a distraction from both: pseudo-Aphrodite of our days.

This one musical-comedy movie[*Cover Girl,* 1944] would be
nothing in itself. But it expresses so many tendencies and lacks
that it is worth approaching. Nothing critical need be said: but
the lack is interesting to us, and the pleasure is worth remembering. There are three rare sequences in the film: a performance
on a very small stage (an Army truck) of one of the best paro-
dies of four or five comedy routines ever recorded, for speed and
violence of timing; a love scene, which is wordless and danced,
a slow tango of the hero and heroine among the empty tables
piled with upturned chairs of a closed and empty nightclub; and
the wordless dance of conflict. The strong identification of the
audience can be felt during the two dramatic scenes by everyone in the theater: the comedy of the third sequence is such that
the sound track is lost in the enormous laughter.

There is nothing of the level of these three scenes in the rest of the film. Language has not been used at all: the conversation is the flattest, most uniform imaginable, in all the other sequences.

SONGS OF CHILDREN

There are ways in which poetry reaches the people who, for one reason or another, are walled off from it. Arriving in diluted forms, serving to point up an episode, to give to a climax an intensity that will carry it without adding heaviness, to travel toward the meaning of a work of graphic art, nevertheless poetry does arrive. And in the socially accepted forms, we may see the response and the fear, expressed without reserve, since they are expressed during enjoyment which has all the sanctions of society.

Close to song, poetry reaches us in the music we admit: the radio songs that flood our homes, the jukeboxes, places where we drink and eat, the songs of work for certain occupations, the stage-songs we hear as ticketed audience.

Even before music, in the rhythm-songs of children, the change-about of key words makes the texture of song. Music is not separated from non-music, in the large world of childhood; the running of the word, the imitative noises, the early groupings and *portamento* sounds are part of an experience which is fluid. In a study of the music of young children, Gladys Evelyn Moorhead and Donald Pond say that over and over again they have seen a child's activities take their course, speech becoming song or chant or speech once more, movement merging into rhythmic sound and returning again to movement, musical instruments being played and discarded without any break or change in the essential character of the activity. It is not possible for the observer to make a sharp distinction between speech and song.

In the same way, certainly, it is not possible while watching children to make a distinction between play and work; and, from Vico on, this lack of distinction has reminded the perceptive of poetry. The little child I watch will take a car that fits his hand and run it up the long hill of a chair-back, making an uphill sound, and then a babble of syllables signifying "car" and "up" and signifying his pleasure most of all. That this is work and learning is so; but to anyone listening who is willing to put away the grown-up distinctions and impatiences, it is also, and primarily, an expression: the sound and the act both "meaning" car-and-up; or, perhaps, something like up-sounds-car.

These little children will let you feel the pleasure with which they prolong the syllables when they know, say, thirty of them. Later, their statements will be sung; and the statement of one, "I have a red chair," will be taken up, and repeated by others in chant form, as the pleading and response will gather against the hum and mutterings of a Virginia congregation, raised to a religious and creative moment and joining to form a song, to make flower—rather than compose—a spiritual.

Neither among the children nor in the congregation—devoted and mature—is there a question of composition, nor of a split between work and play, devotion and form. With the children, form is unknown. None of the limits are acknowledged; one cannot speak in terms of freedom, T. S. Eliot would say. "There is no freedom in art," he believes; "freedom is only freedom when it appears against the background of an artificial limitation."

If the children are expressing possibility and not limitation, may not the congregation be seen as expressing spiritual limitation? And may not the background of art be precisely that consciousness of spiritual limitation?— which can be translated into formal terms at any moment?

Now the songs which children are taught to sing are unlike the songs they make. We learn that a four-line, rhymed verse, carrying some narrative, is the first. Songs that are fit: measured, "story" songs:

Early in the morning, down by the station,
See the little puffer-billies all in a row;
See the little driver turn his little engine;
Piffity-piff! Choo-choo! Off we go!

is closer, in its feeling, and sound imitation, and pointing "See" than most of the small ballads. But the children's own music is likely to sing:

Da da da da da da da da. Pea-nuts.

or

You can't catch me. You can't catch me.

or

Along comes the steamboat and the
person comes walking down the street. And the
water comes right down and shows the man.
Ah...man. Yah yah yah dow ba
bee oh ah bah ah oh ah nay nay
yow oh nah nah.

The child's sense of simplicity, his complex consciousness of rhythm, and in fact his concepts, cannot be satisfied or judged by adult standards. He is interested in things as themselves, he requires that rhythms "be dynamic and generated by impulses which he can feel," in the words of Moorhead and Pond. The child is not concerned with what he should feel. Adults look for melodic unsophistication, rhythmic uncomplexity, and lack of harmonic subtlety, and long to impose a program on the music.

They serve as middlemen; and the function of the middleman is to select so that the audience conforms to his ideas, whether his position be as movie executive, publisher, advertising art director, or a grown-up introducing his early songs to a child.

There is no tradition of the songs of children from two to six. We do know many of the songs that have been sung to babies and little children; the Provençal songs, and the Spanish lullabies, as Lorca transcribed them, and the sacred lullabies of Europe are timeless and evocative, and one may understand a great deal, in singing them, about early music; and also why the French say instead of "go to sleep," "make sleep." In English, now, we do not have many lullabies. We know "Rockabye Baby" and "Bye-bye, Baby Bunting" and the carols; and the Gershwins' "Summertime."

"Summertime" is a song that bridges several traditions: it is an example of a verse that reaches back to English lullaby, to the Southern Negro women who brought up the children, Negro and white; and to the binding influence of self-conscious, American Jewish, trained artists—one a musician, one a lyric-writer—that would produce for a successful Broadway opera the song beginning:

> Summertime,
> An' the livin' is easy,
> Fish are jumpin'
> An' the cotton is high—
> Oh yo' daddy's rich
> An' yo' ma is good-lookin',
> So hush, little baby,
> Don' yo' cry....

with the opposites implicit in its lines and in the high slow composite melody.

THE BLUES: HANDY, LEADBELLY,
JELLY ROLL MORTON, BESSIE SMITH

Clearest among the traditions of poetry in our music is that of the blues. In Abbe Niles' classic introduction to Handy's book, the illiteracy of their makers is mentioned first: they were barroom pianists, careless nomadic laborers, watchers of trains and steamboats, streetcorner guitar players, and whores. They were outcasts, says the book. What must first be said is that they were Negroes in the South. They had known the spirituals and work songs, John Henry and Joe Turner were their important people and their songs were the background. So was the Mississippi, Storyville, and Beale Street. So also were the French and Italian operas, and Beethoven. You have to remember W. C. Handy, not old and feted as I saw him, but after the panic of 1893, leading the orchestra in selections from Beethoven's Fifth in the afternoon, and numbers by Paul Dresser and Charles K. Harris at night. In 1903, Handy got his own band together, and, one of those days, outside a country station, he heard some-body playing a guitar with a knife blade and singing something about "where the Southern cross the Dog." That bit and his jot-ting of the tune turned into "Yellow Dog," with its ending:

> Easy Rider's got to stay away, so he
> Had to vamp it, but the hike ain't far,—
> He's gone where the Southern cross the Yellow Dog.

If the song were printed verse, a cry of "obscurity!" would rise. There is one kind of "obscurity"—that is, a reference to private images, which are private only because the poem is badly writ-ten and the image in question has not been prepared for, in any of the ways of musical or verbal approach which can be achieved in a poem. Another complaint will come from an audience either outside of a group culture or not wishing to be exposed to a novelty which might for a moment cause them to lose their equilibrium. Syntax can be as great a novelty here as any other. But, in these songs, the references are very plain, and known to an entire—whether or not "outcast"—society. It would be easy for a visiting lecturer to ask what the title "Tiger Rag" or "Rum Boogie" means; and he might very well be told. In the same way, it would be easy enough to find out that an easy rider is the pimp who is the whore's true lover, that "to vamp" refers to shoes and means "to walk," and that the ending describes Morehead, Mississippi, where the Yazoo Delta Railroad crosses the Southern lines.

The blues is a method. It represents a treatment of songs, first by W. C. Handy, and then by a great line of singers and musicians. That it includes its minor thirds, its subdominant modulations, its tragic despair and its edge of sharpened humor—all of this is true; it also includes its own verse form and, by now, a rich uncollected literature of song. On the records and in the songbooks, in the sheets and the critiques, you will find every riff, every trumpet solo and break, every detail of orchestration, analyzed. Almost nothing has been said about the words. Both Sterling Brown and Langston Hughes have written, in their own poems and in prose, about the blues and their scenes and significance; but the amazing mixture of keen poetry and vulgarization has never come into our texts, either for what it is or for its influence on our poetry.

It is easy to see the colors of other song-literature on our poems. The Border ballads above all have set their magic and their formal base into the foundation of English and American poetry. The *lieder* and Heine's lyrics have entered our tradition; and the Elizabethan lyric as Shakespeare, Peele, and Jonson knew it. Lorca, particularly in translation, has left an odd, unassimilated trace on images and lines of poets writing English without any real idea of

THE "USES" OF POETRY

what the *romancero* was to him, or the *cante jondo*. But these songs
which are deep in our years and memories—with the "St. Louis
Blues" as fountainhead—are hardly recorded as influence.

They are present to us, and the poetry is in the lines of these
blues and folksongs, from "TB Blues" with its timeless

Too late, too late, too late, too late, too late;

and Leadbelly's "New York City":

When I get to Louisiana, gonna walk and tell,
New York City is a burnin' hell.

The ballad that Leadbelly made about Bill Martin and Ella Speed
lets the description in, with its moments of talk among the verses.
His shouts about Washington, his talkin' blues, like "Roberta,"
in which he sings:

Way up de river, far as I can see,
I thought I spied my ol-time used-to-be.

and then, speaking:

He looked, an' he thought he spied de steamboat comin'.
But it wasn' nothin' but a cypress tree.

or the song, "Blind Lemon," about Blind Lemon Jefferson, the
early singer and guitar player who taught Josh White, and
Leadbelly himself, and many others.

Another singer whose blues enter into our tradition is Jelly
Roll Morton, whose

I'm the winnin' boy, don't deny my name

has one of the most subtle and haunting effects of all our songs.

Bessie Smith is the great voice of this song. "Young Woman's Blues," with

> *See that long lonesome road—*
> *Lord, you know it's got to end—*

is one of the monuments of those seasons and their people. Her blues, too, is the one beginning,

> *He left me at midnight, clock was striking twelve—*

and the countless others which have been carried on by singers now living, or preserved among the many records Bessie Smith made, which today are re-issued or collectors' items. Her life acts out these songs; with her Tennessee childhood, the discovery by Ma Rainey and the nights singing in barns and tents; the bronze, full woman, pushing away the microphone, her power and implacable richness matched only by the great singers—the wealth in New York, the stage shows and floods of drink, the despair in her songs and in her failures, and the final agony when after an accident in Mississippi in 1937, the hospital turned her away because she was not white, and she bled to death after the frantic ride and the waiting for her turn at the second hospital. In full possession of their triumph and their song, their powers realized, these singers in a moment are surrounded by the doorless walls of an ambivalent society. When a door is made, and the unnumbered eyes shine from behind the wall, the song is proved. We have seen it, as we look in dread away from that hospital, to a courtroom in San Francisco or to that day before the Lincoln Memorial in Washington when Marian Anderson, denied a hall, sang human realization in the open air. The poetry is in these songs, not only the art songs, but the spirituals and the blues. It is in the "Death Sting Me Blues" that Sara Martin sings, which opens,

> O come all you women and listen to my tale of woe.

It is impossible, surely, to separate these songs from their music. In some of them, the words are nothing—as the words of many of the best songs are—without the unity of song. But Robert Goffin has said that jazz music is "pure and clean," and that the lyrics are "impure and dirty." The truth is otherwise.

Descended as they are from spirituals, they do not have the sacred declaration of

> Well, they pierced him in the side, in the side, in the side,
> Well, they pierced him in the side and the blood come
>   a-twinkalin' down,
> Well, they pierced him in the side, and the blood come
>   a-twinkalin' down.
> Then he hung down his head, and he died.

But from those peaks of devotional song, we get the transition into the daily fact of this:

> Our Father, who art in heaven, White man owe me 'leven,
>   and pay me seven,
> Thy Kingdom come, Thy will be done, And if I hadn't
>   tuck that, I wouldna' got none.

And the roots going back to the slave songs "Link O' Day" and "Didn't My Lord Deliver Daniel," with the marvelous verses:

> *He delivered Daniel from the lions' den,*
> *Jonah from the belly of the whale,*
> *And the Hebrew chillun from the fiery furnace,*
> *And why not every man?...*
>
> *De moon run down in a purple stream,*
> *The sun forbear to shine,*
> *And every star disappear—*
> *King Jesus shall be mine.*

And the Kentucky song, "O Death!...O death! Can't you spare me over for another year?"

The cowboy songs, like "The Streets of Laredo"; mining songs. I think of "Down, Down, Down"; the haunting "Shenandoah," which began as a land ballad and was taken up as a chantey; "Black, Black, Black," an adaptation of the English song; and strike songs like "Pie in the Sky" and the modern "Joe Hill"—these are the songs that have come into our lives.

The innovations are not here, but in songs like "See See Rider" (whose title is another form of "Easy Rider"):

> *See see rider see what you done done to me—Lawd, Lawd!*

and songs like "Fifty-Two Ladies in Sea-Green Pajamas," which sounds improbably close to Wallace Stevens; and "I Know Your Wig Is Gone," and Jimmy Durante's Umbriago songs, with their decorative and direct and "obscure" humor. And in the popular songs; in the lines from "You're the Top":

> *You're the National Gallery.*
> *You're Garbo's salary,*
> *You're Cellophane—*

In jazz, too, we have the approximation to the "abstract poetry" that *transition* used to teach. As long as words are used, there is no abstract poetry. Words are both abstract and concrete, and, used in relation, can never be abstract. If one word made a song, it might be called abstract. And there is Christian Morgenstern's truly abstract poem, "Night Song of the Fish," which is here reprinted entire:

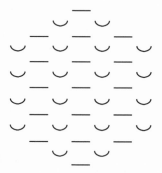

There is a poem that should suit the most exacting. Any praise can be given it: its content and its form are inextricably joined, and perfectly suited to each other; it is pure poetry; it is traditional, and experimental. It is The Lyric.

The syllabic singing which has been called "scat" and "bop" is extremely popular now, and, as far as I know, always has been. There are examples of the same syllabic songs in medieval students' notes, and I am sure we are on the road back to incantation—or, full circle, to the game-songs of children, used to set a rhythm in motion. The repetition of tones, or of syllables, does produce a trance-like condition, as does the watching of a rhythmic motion such as perfect oscillation. Helmholtz says, in his basic study of tone, that water in motion has an effect similar to that of music; the motion of waves, rhythmic and varied in detail, produces the feelings of repose or weariness—and, he adds, reminds us of order and power and the fine links of life.

Meter, in poetry, is allied to these effects and the long search for their causes. We begin to believe that there are resonances according to which the body responds, in its rhythms, to external motion and rhythm. Beyond that, the connections by which we may identify because of rhythm are beginning to be made. In a series of tests, it was discovered that very few people recognized their own hands or feet or profile views, but that when they were shown a film in which they could see themselves walking (even when the face was not shown), they could identify with their own rhythms, and recognize themselves. In this recognition, both empathy and memory present new possibilities. We know that memory has a great deal to do with the power of poetry. We know that verse has a certain value as a mnemonic device. This value depends partly on the rhythm itself; partly on the meter, the segmenting of rhythm into measurable parts; and partly on the sounds, not even of the words this time, but of the syllables.

In prose, the search may be for the *mot juste*; if you allow the concept of the ideal, in poetry you will have to search for the right word, yes, but you will have to go farther, and find the sound *juste*. You are dealing with the sounds themselves, as resonances, as the syllables of words laden with association, and as quantitative and qualitative units. We are close to music, here, and we are not allowed to forget the songs, whether our poems are for the page or part of a sung and spoken folklore.

SILENCE AND PUNCTUATION

The silences, here, are part of the sound. In the melodic music. Working on film, one deals with time; part of the data is the rate at which the projector functions, the number of seconds per foot of film at which the image track and the sound track are shown. When one is transcribing sound for film, the pauses may be indicated by time. And in a song, too, the pauses are indicated.

In the printed poem, the punctuation has an importance which all too frequently has not been given it. Many poets, and of course many students, will say that they have no patience with punctuation: they "cannot punctuate" as they "cannot spell." But, as you realize when you hear a poet read his own work, the line in poetry—whether it be individual or traditional—is intimately bound with the poet's breathing. The line cannot go against the breathing-rhythm of the poet.

Punctuation is biological. It is the physical indication of the body-rhythms which the reader is to acknowledge; and, as we know it, punctuation in poetry needs several inventions. Not least of all, we need a measured rest. Space on the page, as E. E. Cummings uses it, can provide roughly for a relationship in emphasis through the eye's discernment of pattern; but we need a system of pauses which will be related to the time-pattern of the poem. I suggest a method of signs equivalating the metric foot and long and short rests within that unit. For spoken poetry, for poems approaching song, and indeed for the reading of any of these—since we are never without the reflection of sound which exists when we imagine words—a code of pauses would be valuable.

SONG AND POEM

To receive from song all that it may give would be to bring new gifts to poetry. Even in commercial songwriting, with its continual appraisal of an artificial target—"the public" thought of as apart from "the people"—flickers of imagery and lyricism rise, and make themselves felt. The long line that goes against our popular song tradition has come into two wildly popular songs this year; but it is not their technical skills, nor even what they do, so much as what they lack, that allows song-verse and radio-verse to keep its relaxation as amusement art. It never includes the fertility of our range; in seeming to sing love, or in seeming to sing poverty, it sings distraction.

And the songs and poems, used on radio, throw away the gift of the isolated voice. Radio poetry could now make its leap, could enter a level in which the single voice, or a very few voices, might invite an opening-up of consciousness undefined by the other senses. The eye, and the impressions we receive by being a member of a large audience in a place that is of necessity a social place, bring their own demands. The requirements of comparative privacy—the home, a room where a radio is—can offer another kind of poetry that has not yet been imagined.

But all our arts of song offer this: a young poetry not yet born. The vitality and sense of triumph in our singing have this promise; the emptiness of its relation to the needs of the people have turned it away again and again. The singing arts are ready for poetry. Perhaps it is their joy that will invite the poems.

I think of a story about the last day of the Jewish lunar month, at the end of which a blessing on the new moon must be made. Once, at the end of Yom Kippur, the sky was cloudy, the moon could not be seen. The Baal Shem Tov tried in his holiness with all his powers of concentration to make the moon come out. Outside, the Hasidim were celebrating: they danced and rejoiced, until they burst into the room of the Baal Shem Tov, at first dancing before him, and then drawing him into the dance. Suddenly, in the dance, someone called, "The moon is out!" They all ran out to bless the new moon.

And the holy man said, "What I could not do through my concentration, they have done through their joy."

CHAPTER EIGHT

THE DARKENING OF THE HOUSE

The darkening of the house. The ring of lights overhead, the lamps on the walls, beginning to dim, the profiles down the row calming, becoming luminous, and then shadowed. The last little shriek of laughter, the clearing of the throat, so that you know just what is going on in the stranger, arranging himself to be an "audience." Now darkness, with a leap, as the house lights sink completely. The angels of the proscenium, repainted a fashionable off-white, evade, soar, disappear. There is a ripple across the curtain, and it shivers. It begins to rise, showing a foot of brightly lit floor.

How is it with you, sitting beside me? Our coats are thrown back over the chairs, the little books of the program are on our laps, we almost touch each other's arms in these seats which are not wide enough nor spaced at all, we share an armrest, we breathe this air in which the excitement of the young and the diffused after-dinner preoccupations fuse, in which the air beats with a perfume and a trembling and a mixed hope. The curtain is up, and a landscape is beginning to talk to us. Things are beginning to explain themselves to us. Some people, standing well above the orchestra chairs, grouped so the balcony may understand, are beginning to justify what they have been doing.

That curtain went up with a disclosing motion, the motion of a letter being slid from its envelope. The letter of a stranger? If it is, there will be no strangeness by the time it is half-known. Of a friend? There will be news.

You sit beside me in the house-dark, with the light thrown from the stage on your face, and shadows at your back. When you laugh, I feel it, and I feel the man in front of me throw himself back in his seat and stiffen his back when the dangers make themselves apparent. And then a breaker of laughter runs through all these rows, and seethes itself out, in relief. But we are not separate from the play; we are not a producer's idea of box office take, of the familiar fan-shaped chart of theater seats—not that only. We sit here, very different each from the other, until the passion arrives to give us our equality, and to make us part of the play, to make the play part of us. An exchange is being effected.

Backstage in a theater once, I heard the director speak to the assembled cast. It was opening night. The dress rehearsal had felt good, and during the weak places, many pointed phrases made me see where this—my first play—creaked at the joints, where I needed to understand more. But the director was speaking now: that last minute of talk to the actors and the electricians, the people in charge of music, those responsible for the revolving of the stage. "You have had good equipment to work with," the words came, after the praise and excitement and the sense of courage, "you've had a theater with everything you needed, and you are involved with the play; but all the way through, you have been handicapped. One essential has been denied you. Tonight the audience is there; now they are sitting out front; you have everything you need...."

That was Hallie Flanagan, talking to a group of professionals and apprentices. What she said moved a whole period of work and rehearsal into focus.

But they are moving on their stage. But they are lives; they are moving toward each other; they are promises, and their promise is action; they are threats, and their threats are action. And they speak; and they are silent.

EVERYTHING YOU NEED

The plays of the contemporary theater have had a curious sparseness, and this has been diagnosed many times. Blame has been laid on the movies, for usurping an old art; on the attitude that declares the theater to be a business and not an art; on the uneasiness of the audience, which will spend five dollars for a bottle of whisky and not a pair of seats.

The movies have not usurped the place of the theater, any more than the novel has "usurped" the place of poetry, or science the place of belief. It has been pointed out that "not only does one cultural facility seem never to supersede another, but," as Harvey Fergusson writes, "facilities that once had practical and necessary value tend to be kept alive as cultural facilities when their practical value is largely lost." He looks at horseback riding—a "growing cult"—with the automobile used for practical purposes; the bicycle and the long bow—of which he says there are more in America now than there were when Columbus landed. The statistics can be taken apart; these figures always prove simply that there is now *more* of everything; and the universe of "practical values," in which objects wear out, is not the universe of art.

Our theater is not as good as it has to be; it is corrupted and weakened, split, diluted, gone stale for lack of invention. I speak here of the plays which, in America, we have been able to see and read; and, primarily, of the Broadway theater, that industry which distributes plays to the rest of the country after they have passed the tests of dilutions and re-workings which are intended to make them palatable to a hypothetical public—the ideal "audience" of middlemen, a customer by the thousand, conceived cynically and brutally, a cynical ideal.

The pressure of the movies will have to mean to the theater that new discoveries be made. Novelty here will include the older plays, seen fresh for us by the living—as Shakespeare, Euripides, Ibsen, Strindberg may be seen again, played cumulatively, speaking to generations.

But these are not examples of a present theater. When they are played, they throw into harsh relief one of the symptoms of weakness.

We can trace one illness of our theater in terms of lack of language.

THE LANGUAGE OF OUR THEATER

At this juncture, I wish to defend the wordless—the mute act, which proves itself without speech, which declares and insinuates in silence, and is stamped on memory. Even in concern for poetry, we realize the life of the unspoken. It appears today as a look from one; the slow turning of the body of another, filled with recognition; the stroke of the club, brought down on the head of the man in the subway; the uninterrupted fall of the boy, leaping to safety before a height of fire; the announcement of this body in the stiffness and discolor of death; the bend of the child's head, seeing for the first time roses.

There is no better place than a book about poetry to praise the untold. I praise it; I think of the many moments in music or in action, remembered in their clarity. The personal moments, in their rooms or their fields or their cars, where there were no words, and could not be. Or in drama and movies: in *The Sea Gull*, with the mother bandaging her son's wounded head, so that all the meaning between them, of which the wound was one token, stood clear; in *Children of Paradise*, at the end, with Baptiste fighting through, fighting a sea of carnival, which many-thrusted worked against him, while receding and receding went Garance.

In the arts of speech, however—in poetry and song and the dramatic arts—while silence may be even the climax, it is language and the relations of language with which we deal.

The language of our theater is now so barren, so inadequate to what it is asked to do, that it may be taken as part of the fear of poetry. The dullness of many of our most notable plays is phenomenal; if a certain snob reaction keeps that dullness from being discussed in print, it does not disguise the conversational reaction. Apart from a philistine disavowal, there is a sense of betrayal, not so much by the characters—since action can express a certain amount of the motion of a play—but by the playwright.

In our best-made plays, the resistance to language has taken a few very consistent forms. Never, in these plays, does one need to ask for "poetic" scenes, and of course I do not mean to ask for scenes in which language takes the function of overt action. But language is the chief means of action on the stage. Its other action is defined by language. As a matter of fact, we all know most action is taboo according to the convention of the stage; if you think past the moments at which the scene-curtains fall, you will remember that you have seen nothing—a suggestion of fighting, a kiss, a stylized dance of approach and separation is what we see played out in the Western theater.

A few of the playwrights whose work has been before us during these years have used one device when the action of their plays insisted on language. This is a very curious device, and it makes a curious judgment about "the audience." We have pointed out the growing colorlessness of American speech; the accepted spoken language has trimmed itself of images, diluted the figures, flattened the contours of old-country borrowings. And this emerges in our plays during their moments of heightening, when the gifts of language are necessary. These arrive, but in broken English.

In O'Neill's plays, recently, the sense of imitated speech has been exaggerated. The feeling of drunkenness has been held, in *The Iceman Cometh*, by repeated phrases, a lurching of speech, and the emergence of the Biblical, lyric line then comes through as distortion, with Hugo saying:

> *The days grow hot, O Babylon! 'Tis cool beneath thy*
> *villow trees!*

Even in *Mourning Becomes Electra*, with its impact of emotions thrown against each other, the moment at the waterside, one of the most intense in contemporary theater, belongs to the drunken Chanteyman, who is heard singing the piercing "Shenandoah":

> *Oh Shenandoah I long to hear you—*
> *A-way my rolling river!—*
> *...So early in the morning*
> *The sailor likes his bottle oh—*

And then, after calling for a drink to be bought, he feels in his pocket for his ten dollars. It is gone; he has been rolled by the "yaller-haired pig with the pink dress on"— and he cries, grandson of Melville's men, "Hard down! Heavy gales around Cape Stiff! All is sunk but honor, as the feller says, an' there's damn little o' that afloat!"

Saroyan uses his musicians in the same way, the interruption of music and the repetition of "no foundation!"

And Lillian Hellman shows the situation to us in its fullness, in *Watch on the Rhine*, when in Act Two, Kurt begins to sing, in

German, the song which became that of the German soldiers in the streets of Madrid, on their way to fight for republican Spain. Speaking of that day, eighteen years after the song of Berlin, Kurt says:

> We felt good that morning. You know how it is to be good when it is needed to be good? So we had need of new words to say that. I translate with awkwardness, you understand.

> *And so we have met again.*
> *The blood did not have time to dry.*
> *We lived to stand and fight again.*
> *This time we fight for people....*
> *This time, no farewell, no farewell.*

Extremely moving as it is, heard, this is the extreme to which language, as one material of drama, is relied on in some representative plays.

Thornton Wilder uses another method to make the dimension which language gives the stage. In *The Skin of Our Teeth*, he takes us through the rehearsal of the hours of the night, allowing us to get used to the passages from Spinoza, Plato, and Aristotle, to hear the objections of the cast to phrases they do not understand, and then to call up memory and understanding as we hear the now-familiar lines for the second time. In the other climaxes of the play, he depends on a stirring colloquial speech, which serves its purpose in Act One, when Mr. Antrobus, in despair at the nearness of the glacier, calls to have the fires put out.

> *Mrs. Antrobus:* George, remember all the other times. When the volcanoes came right up in the front yard. And

the time the grasshoppers ate every single leaf and blade
of grass, and all the grain and spinach you'd grown with
your own hands. And the summer there were earth-
quakes every night.

Mr. Antrobus: Henry! Henry! Myself! All of us, we're covered with blood.

Mrs. Antrobus: Then remember all the times you were
pleased with him and when you were proud of yourself.
Henry! Henry! Come here and recite to your father the
multiplication table that you do so nicely.

Until, after the children have recited and sung, Mrs. Antrobus
can say:

Build up the fire. It's cold. Build up the fire. We'll do what
we can. At least the young ones may pull through.

In these moments, when nothing is resolved, the hurried, broken progressions seem appropriate. They are less adequate in the
third act, when the issues of all the war between father and son,
the struggle in which Mr. Antrobus and the son (the fascist,
Henry, Cain) are made to realize that they go on in the world
together. In a moment of profound conflict, which for the audience is a resolution, the language that could carry emotion and
understanding beyond its present is not used, and there is a
relaxation, a sagging, that does a disservice to the play. This break
comes in terms of meaning, which is drama in crisis.

The plays of Odets, again, use the flavor of English spoken with
Jewish inflection, in the rhythms of Hebrew and Yiddish. Robert
Sherwood has done a different thing with the meanings of his
plays; he has twice changed the basic attitudes of plays to suit them
to the pressures of the moment, re-writing the ending of *Idiot's*

Delight and changing the scene of *There Shall Be No Night*. This is mentioned for its interest as one attitude that a writer has had toward his material. That this writer was head of the Foreign Branch of the Office of War Information is of interest, also, since both of these plays dealt with the meanings of war, and the writer felt that his original meanings would not stand.

For of course the language of the theater is also its meaning, although the action—the pantomime—may not be misinterpreted for a moment, nor its function slighted. There has been in our time a lack of reliance on language and a lack of experimentation which are frightening to anyone who sees them as symptoms. We know the phenomenon of stage-fright: it holds the player shivering, incapable of speech or action. Perhaps there is an audience-fright which the playwright can feel, which leaves him with these incapacities.

T. S. Eliot has said that the "ideal medium for poetry...is the theater." Surely this is true; as surely, work with the audience will have to be done before the theater of poetry emerges, say the producers. The audience will stay away in thousands if a play is advertised as a "poetic drama," they say. They are thinking of advertising, promotion, and the reviews based on them; this is a custom of the middleman.

Is there any truth here?

The "poetic theater" has been happy, for the businesmen, the artists, the audience. From the best to the most diluted, "successes" have arrived: without regard to their value as art, one may look at the records of various productions of *Hamlet*, *Cyrano de Bergerac*, *Winterset*, *Medea*. There have also been the plays which enter printed literature, whatever becomes of them on the stage: Cummings' *him*; Eliot's *Murder in the Cathedral*, *Family Reunion*, and *The Rock*; Jeffers' *The Tower Beyond Tragedy* and *Dear Judas*; Auden's *The Dog Beneath the Skin*, *The Ascent of F-6*, and *The*

Dance of Death; MacLeish's *Panic*, and his radio plays; the stage works of Maxwell Anderson, Edna St. Vincent Millay, and Alfred Kreymborg, which are in another category; and the work of such masters as Yeats, Synge, Shaw, Brecht, Pirandello, and of all those others whose great plays have entered our language to show us what is and what might be.

There is one writer who has let language emerge as action recently: Tennessee Williams, a playwright and a poet, has ranged from the blue piano and the Mexican woman intoning, *"Flores. Flores. Flores para los muertos. Flores. Flores...."* to the streaming soliloquies of danger and the abrupt shifts of seduction and violence, in all of which the inner action and the outer are equilibrated by means of language. Sometimes false, often hypnotic and inescapable, these speeches extend the action of his plays, giving them a density, setting up a world, which is too many times absent from the theater. Lillian Hellman will do this by implication, in her precisely controlled scenes of antagonism; in packed lines, each phrase of which goes backward and backward to remind and warn us. In *Another Part of the Forest*, one of these close-filled lines in which time, an image of the far and marvelous Greece, learned behind a driven mule, and the convoluted relation of father and daughter, are held, in a speech really about approaching marriage:

Maybe next year, or the year after, you and I'll make that trip to Greece, just the two of us.

These speeches sound specific; they are more. They open up memory and discovery, as the moments of language and the theater do. In Arthur Miller's writing, which counts on an effect of flatness that is to be found in most of our well-made fiction in this period, the question is used for a kind of sonority, a reverberation of con-

sciousness that actually demands more consciousness and more language. After the inarticulateness of most of his people, we feel relief
when a man breaks through and cries to another man:

> Don't you live in the world? What the hell are you?...
> What must I do to you?

DANCE, PANTOMIME, A JUGGLER, THE DIVINE SERVICE

The experimental theater has been freer. It has, sometimes,
welcomed the freeing of language. The Federal Theater moved
in this direction: Marc Blitzstein worked with script and music,
and his declarative statements and his wordless love song
("Francie, Francie") found a reception for their meaning and
their form. Orson Welles was far on the way to a theater that
would relish poetry and give it the excitement and physical life
it is ready to give. His *Caesar* and *Faustus* were landmarks of a
generation. We need to go on from this lost theater; it remembered many things while it was doing many things. As Robert
Edmond Jones has written, "Does this mean that we are to carry
images of poetry and vision and high passion in our minds while
we are shouting out orders to electricians on ladders in light
rehearsals? Yes. This is what it means."

What steps may be taken? The stage may be given language.

And, on the other extreme, it may be given dance. One of the
few explorations of the last years has been made not by the theater of plays, but by the musical-comedy theater, which, for all
its stupidities, may be closer to being usable than the weakened
theater. In the best recent musicals, the dance has been used for
exposition. Ballets have taken the place of the maid and the
confidante; the mechanical introduction to a scene has been
scrapped. The significance of this is apparent. I have talked about
the use of language, but the set speeches, made directly to the

audience by someone who pretends to be speaking to another person of the play, were a dead convention. This failure was superseded by a full acting-out of the information, made directly to the audience in pantomime and dance. The range is infinite: the Civil War was indicated by the ballet in *Bloomer Girl,* and there has been a dance on the burlesque stage in which a love scene was danced, contrapuntally and most curiously, by a dancer dressed half as a man and half as a woman. The Marx brothers have acted out elaborate puns, and jokes based on his almost exclusively verbal humor have been conveyed by Harpo Marx, who with Charles Chaplin, Jimmy Savo, and Danny Kaye, ranks as a master artist of pantomime. And I have seen the juggler Stan Cavanaugh convey with the rhythms of his juggling such fervor and gaiety as was intelligible to an audience of many hundreds; they laughed as children do, with pleasure and delight, identifying with the rhythms and the risk.

The dance itself has attempted again to assume language. This step comes next; poems and plays too can find their forms, freeing themselves once more. Martha Graham, essaying Emily Dickinson, is one of many dancers who has begun to work with poetry. Anna Sokolow, Jane Dudley, have begun experiments. Thurber's stories, Lorca's poems—there is range here, from musical comedy to a most hieratic form, from the talk of Fred Astaire, beginning to tap, to the religious dance and chant of the Indian rituals.

Tribal chant has come through very little. One looks in vain for additions to the divine services of the religious now practiced in this country. In music, work has been commissioned: both Bloch and Milhaud have written services which are now being played, but the traditional words of the service were preserved. It might be well to suggest to the more exploratory churches and temples that they collaborate with writers to find forms to carry on their worship.

ı

The poetry of the Bible has been emphasized, due largely to Moulton's work in the literary study of the Bible, and to the various recent editions of the Bible which offer the poetry—prophecies, the books of poems and songs, and the poetry which has appeared as blocks of prose—printed in its own lines. The strong tradition of parallel verse, as present to many of us as the French and English forms, is a vital influence in poetry and in prose, and work with the Bible is marvelously fertile, in music and in symbols as well as in meaning. The way in which belief is written in these books is the best answer to many of the artificial questions about form and content, technique and emotion. These answers are rarely heard, but they make the false dualities wither away.

Barriers dissolve, too, when confronted by the Eastern poems: the poems of the sacred books, in Yeats' translation of the Upanishads, or Isherwood's of the Bhagavad-Gita, and such work as E. Powys Mathers' *Black Marigolds* and Robert Payne's *The White Pony*, a rich anthology of Chinese poetry.

RADIO AND THE VOID: THE ARTICULATE

Among the false distinctions that go down is the distinction between written and spoken poetry. Among the radio programs now broadcast, and the records being issued, are several which use poetry at its best and most accessible. I think of T. S. Eliot's new recording of *The Waste Land*, and the reissue of Edith Sitwell's *Façade*, with music by William Walton.

And past and future meet in some of these. Radio poetry is not yet born, although many poets have believed that reading for broadcast would cause the forms to rise. MacLeish, Corwin, and some others have approached the many-voiced structure that might be set against a single narrator's or poet's voice. But neither the form nor the faith emerged. In radio, we see the old Taoist meaning: The Taoist meaning which says that the vessel is *the void and the vessel*; the bowl is *the void and the bowl enclosing it*; the window is *the void and the window framing it*. The radio is the void, and the voice which fills it; as far as poetry goes, it is there to be found. Past and future are in it, as I heard past and future meet lately at two meetings. The first was at a Seder, that Passover dinner at which deliverance and the desert which follows deliverance both are celebrated. This is a traditional evening, at which traditional questions are asked, the set answers are made, and the old songs are sung. This night was different from all other nights, however. Another song was sung. Among the ritual, it moved everyone, it made tears start, when the singer began the first low notes of "Let My People Go." It was the first time, the hearers knew, that the spiritual had been sung at that moment, in that place, and a barrier went down before that song.

The other day, I heard a recording of Milhaud's *Orestes*, with Claudel's words. The beaten-out rhythms, the surge as of stroke-singing for a ship, or cheerleading for some illuminated Games, sent a thrill of music through the words. That marvelous pulse has its place in our poems, in our theater, and in our knowledge of what people mean, in their excitement and their articulate dream.

It is a great thing to hear the words of those who are worthy to speak them. It is a great thing to learn this in oneself, sitting in the dim rows at the play, shedding the tears that do not rise from struggle, but from identifying with another human being created before your eyes; it is a great thing to laugh with pleasure and delight, as children laugh; it is a great thing to say to our wordless, we will speak, in self-knowledge, in faith, at a beginning-place of many beginnings, in which none of these means is enough in itself, since each is an index to a beginning of the single spirit or of the world; it is a great thing to come to the unbegun places of our living and to say: Now we will find the words.

CHAPTER NINE

⊚

THE IMAGISTS AND MENTAL IMAGERY

"We are not a school of painters," said the Imagist poets, "but we believe that poetry should render particulars exactly and not deal in vague generalities, however magnificent and sonorous."

If we, reading an Imagist poem, find those particulars rendered exactly; if the glaze of rain is on the red wheelbarrow; if we know these pines splashed by the sea on our rocks; it is because our powers are like the powers of the poet. It is not only that we see the same colors, not only that we relate the action "splash" to the shape of a pine tree: it is because our total activity and the use of our imagination—whatever our experience—are like those of the artist.

WRITING AND THE "ARTS OF SIGHT"

Now the relation of writing to the arts of sight may be seen in a wide range of forms, from the image lifted out of the poem to the title of a painting; and perhaps most clearly to our time, in films, with the writing that goes into the script and determines the image track, and the dialogue we hear as we "see" the finished movie. There is no word for the audience action before a movie or an opera or a television screen. The combination of sense-actions is too clear; but the lack of a word is true before any of the arts. No one sense is employed in perceiving a work of art, and probably no one sense is ever employed alone. It is easy to say that one reads a poem; we might say also that we read paintings; but nobody ever speaks of reading skywriting; and, in our vernacular, we go to the movies. It might be best to say that we go to a book, and go to a painting.

"I want to tell you about a boat." That was the challenge that Francis Galton used to find out about the strength of mental imagery. He found that no one person would immediately make the image specific far beyond the sharpness of this general word; another person would suppress the imagery altogether, as those who deal in abstractions do, starving their visual faculties. But if the faculty is free in its actions, Galton said, it can select the images it needs, shift them in any way it wishes, and use and take pleasure in its actions. Galton went on, of course, to particularize the boat; and he made the necessary further declaration that the visual power was to be "subordinated to the higher intellectual operations."

A FEW PAINTERS

The connections between writing and painting have been spoken about with the same split and duality that has afflicted our approach to every human act. It has been left to a deprecation of certain paintings for being "literary"; for dealing, if they are representational, with juxtapositions like those at the climax of a dramatic work—or, if they are not, for having pompous and inflated titles that direct the audience to a sentimental associative position.

But to be given paintings whose images make a sense of arrival in us; whose balance reminds us of the rhythms of our dreams as well as of those of waking reality; whose people and whose scenes and whose shapes evoke, through their particulars, that deep recognition and dismay which turns and thanks and changes into love: this is where painting becomes most memorable. And here the sharpness of sight dissolves, evokes experience and memory and dream, journeys through storms of association to become sharp on another level, clear and sharp as sight perfected and capable of many focuses and many perspectives.

I think of specific paintings: of our inheritance of our painting in which the detail is never verified, but whose clarity is all in the emotional impact of seeing and remembering, until these dark abstracted shapes of omen call landscapes to themselves, and recognizable seas, and surf breaking against certain rocks, and a lonely indicated figure setting out on his journey—a journey which grows in a moment, like that sea and that overhang of mountain, to be universal and at hand to all. These are Ryder and Hartley and Barnes: Ryder whose pitch of ocean, whose rolling Jonah and death-horse and splinter of ship among waves and moons continue to arrive in meaning, believing in art, making a tragic and hieratic monument; Marsden Hartley, who under Monadnock lay, and found the Canadian fishermen in their passion, and remembered Ryder in the New York rainstorm, and beat the fountains of surf on the brown stones, and cursed Hemingway for only seeming to strike the penknife into the palm of his hand, for Hartley knew there were many ways to be brave; and Matthew Barnes, painting small, lost and purposive man forever walking under a fiery sky, toward a small house, along water or along the empty magical cliff, until the atom bomb reminded him of the journey, the little shell of a boat pointing out with its one voyager into the sea-fog, the infinite various whiteness.

I think of Ben Shahn and Symeon Shimin—Shahn with his imagined ruins, the pointed people, the red twisted iron of imagined Italy, of his earlier walls, and the crowded color of delicatessen windows, the memorial paintings to Sacco and Vanzetti, and that one scene of the pebble beach, a thousand stones in their uniqueness and precision, across which the soldier lies in his hard brown stained clothes, dead, his foot at a little edge of sea. And Shimin's mural, with its central child, its sleeping boys crumpled against brick, and the stream of factory children with their starving eyes: against whom are given, glowing in color and concentration, the students (a triangle of shoulder and back, an edge of averted face) grouped around the glass vessels, poised over the blueprint's diagram, and the luminous amber of the triangle in the foreground hand, the intermittent brightness raining on the green of a high field, everything meaning the present and everything meaning the chance of the future.

I think of the rays of light around an image by Morris Graves, and the summoning-up of what Japan has given us, in this bird, in this bronze painted on silk; and of the Indian woman against inescapable sun on the dry Mexican mountains that Xavier Guerrero painted; and of the experiment in the South American vaulted hall where Siqueiros made the shapes of women changing as you move through, in "walking perspective." Of Feininger, and Scharl, and Perlin, and Jeanne d'Orge; certain Marins, certain Sheelers, Rivera and Tamayo on the Mexican buildings, Orozco at Dartmouth and Pomona, the Kollwitz of the unforgetting eyes, and the scene of Spain as it reaches us: Guernica, the Catalan Costa Brava.

A GRAPHICS WORKSHOP

During the war, an attempt was made to use writing with the work of some of the painters. In a workshop where Shahn, Perlin, Koerner were among the painters, I served as writer, and many artists were called in; work was commissioned and planned. Welders by Shahn were to be used to remind us of our mixed birth; a head by Shimin, the head of a young Negro boy, for the chance to grow; a landscape by Curry with a line of Whitman's; a raft of three survivors on a copper-hot sea by Peter Blume; a grotesque of syphilis by Dali; the starving children of Käthe Kollwitz. None of these was ever used. Advertising men came in, telling the administration that ideas were their field, that the government needed their techniques. The advertising men made it clear that there were two ways of looking at ideas in a war against fascism. Those of us who were working on the project believed ideas were to be fought for; the advertising men believed they were to be sold. The audience, those at home in wartime, were not "citizens" or "people." They were "customers." No such ideas as ours were to be executed. The advertising men won, with those who decided that this was not a war against fascism, that it was a war to be won, and the meaning worked out afterward. It was at this time that Stevie Smith published in England a poem with the line:

Perhaps America will have an idea, and perhaps not.

The Graphics Workshop was dissolved. I had left it before that time. The story is not an important one. It is a good emblem, however; and among the things we learned was the impact that a combined form may have when picture and text approach the meaning from different starting-places. In this combination of an image and a few words, there are separables: the meaning of the image, the meaning of the words, and a third, the meaning of the two in combination. The words are not used to describe the picture, but to extend its meaning. A few words will have a quality of great directness, if they are appropriate, if they do extend the picture's meaning, and if they are printed in such a way as to confirm the balance of the picture. I am not speaking here of a slogan, which does hammer the heads of the audience in order

to sell an idea, but of few words or many used as text with painting, photograph, or collage. The nature of the words may be
varied, and interest may be sustained throughout a very long passage, if the matter be something of immediate concern—such
as price changes—or if the eye be directed through the text by
its writing and design.

The exhibitions using poems and prose, enlarged to wall dis-
plays and used on the walls of the New York Public Library before
they were sent about the country, were another proof of the value
in reinforcement of paintings—Goya, Daumier, Orozco—and
words from T. S. Eliot and Edith Sitwell to Roosevelt, S. V. Benét,
May Sarton, Whitman, Langston Hughes. Any single contribution might have stood alone. In juxtaposition, they were all set in
motion toward each other.

POSTERS, PHOTOGRAPHS, AND SEQUENCE-WRITING

The two people whose attitudes were an illumination here
were Romana Javitz, whose division, the Picture Collection of
the New York Public Library, has added another definition to the
idea of "book," and E. McKnight Kauffer, whose posters and
paintings and book designs continually suggest new openings for
the combination of word and image.

From the use of writing with paintings to its use with series
of photographs is a larger step than it would appear. Photography
itself is the most accepted graphic art; its immediacy answers the
need that our newspaper readers have for the eye-witness, a
need that runs all through our culture, and has developed the on-
the-spot broadcast as well as Weejee, the photographer of *Naked
City.* Contemporary photography includes the thousands who
will be out the next clear afternoon with their box cameras, and
the thousands who argue in terms of filters and exposure meters
and hypo, as well as Paul Strand and Walker Evans, Ralph Steiner,

Cartier-Bresson, Man Ray, Helen Leavitt, Ansel Adams, and Berenice Abbott. The Saturday arguments about photography as a machine art are answered by the best photographers. "If the camera were a machine!" Berenice Abbott said, "with the precision and the flexibility, the accommodation and power of machines as we know them today!" And "Our lighting has not been begun," she said. "We need a light as good as sunlight— better than sunlight."

But the photographers are used to a certain degree of acceptance, and the symbols of acceptance. The experimenters have all the struggles of novelty to face; but, for the most part, the picture magazines and the picture-book publishers are cordial, although Paul Strand, doing his own printing, must find private backing for his portfolios, and the radical new methods of Berenice Abbott are still unknown. The writing, however, which accompanies the photographs is worn, descriptive, faded writing. The most powerful picture magazine [*Life*], whose editor has developed a style to use elsewhere, prints better and better photographs, while its writing lags a generation behind, and the captions for the photographs repeat the images and are printed in blocks beneath, for all the world like the labels on cans of soup. Their reactionary content aside, this writing is reactionary: it is as if the experiments of the photographs were each time denied by the text.

Two writers, James Agee especially, and Wright Morris, have published books which indicate the fertility of this combination. *Let Us Now Praise Famous Men* is struck with the passion and anger and illumination that attention to the particulars of the life of tenant farmers have given a fine poet and a fine photographer. Most of Walker Evans' photographs were omitted from the book as it has appeared; perhaps that will be remedied, so that a milestone in our literature of meeting-places may fully be seen.

In writing for sequences of stills, the motion of the sequence

is a primary consideration. The editing and arranging of the photographs will determine the flow of the text. The large page of
the popular magazines is a difficult one to design so that the text
will move throughout, giving continuity to separate photographs;
but this difficulty can be used as a challenge, and a single-line
running text evolved. On a smaller page, the size used for books
or pocket magazines, one picture or two at the most will provide a visual unit which will carry, and carry well, a complement
of imaginative writing. The first steps have been taken in these
forms, but, everywhere, editors have grown timid before the
explorations were at all fully made. The pattern is like the game
called Giant Steps: a brave advance is almost inevitably followed
by quick backtracking, generally by dilution and debasement of
the original intention so that more "story" is forced in, or the
whole method is distracted to the will of advertising, which has-
tens to use any fresh method for the selling of products.

The advertising empire is the open apparent grave of form in
writing. The parody of the poet's concern with a piece of writing, word for word, can be seen in an art director's conference—or
its effect felt in almost any magazine or radio advertisement.
Content is only form-deep, in any expression; and in the combination of picture and copy on our billboards, our newspapers, in
every medium, we see what happens when anything may be imitated as a means to an end. A burlesque of education, of painting
and of writing, the instructive terror turned loose by the middleman, all is here.

But even here, the concern is still for the content. We are
never concerned more with form than with content, even if we
allow ourselves the illusion of a separation—except, perhaps, in
skywriting. The watchers on the pavement will look up, following the purposive flight of the plane, charted by the
beginning letters *P* and *E*. And fliers taught this technique will

learn how to use the wind, how to finish the letters evenly, how to fly one-half mile at so many feet altitude for a half-character letter and one mile for a full character. Printers and letterers are taught to design appropriately to their text. In the skywriter, we are displayed the triumph of pure form.

From the single word of the skywriter to the single image of the poster painter—who need not, of course, fill his canvas, his given space—is the formal range. But the middle ground is again the most fertile for the combination. The interest of writing captions for a sequence of still photographs, where the illusion of some motion may be sustained, is only the shadow of another interest.

THE SCREENWRITER AND THE CUTTING ROOM

The continuity of film, in which the writer deals with a track of images moving at a given rate of speed, and a separate sound track which is joined arbitrarily to the image track, is closer to the continuity of poetry than anything else in art. But the heaviness of the collective work on a commercial film, the repressive codes and sanctions, unspoken and spoken, the company-town feeling raised to its highest, richest, most obsessive-compulsive level in Hollywood, puts the process at the end of any creative spectrum farthest from the making of a poem.

At the same time, almost anything that can be said to make the difficulties of poetry dissolve for the reader, or even to make the reader want to deal with those "difficulties," can be said in terms of film. These images are like the action sequences of a well-made movie—a good thriller will use the excitement of timing, of action let in from several approaches, of crisis prepared for emotionally and intellectually, so that you can look back and recognize the way of its arrival; or, better, feel it coming until the moment of proof arrives, meeting your memory and your recognition.

The cutting of films is a parable in the motion of any art that lives in time, as well as a parable in the ethics of communication. (I say "ethics" because of the values and obligations involved; I am for a moment discarding the general role of the movie-makers, their studied forgetting of most passion and most interpretation, their rigid definition of the emotional status of their audience and the way in which, like grown-ups prescribing music mechanically for stupid children, they prescribe certain series of emotions and acts whose meanings are not to be questioned.)

The scene is familiar: the cameras set up in the great hangars of studios, the players spotlit in their little corner of a darkness loaded with painted flats and ropes and girders; the signal to shoot, the hush as the cameras note an exchange lasting, say, two minutes; the ending; the repeat; the many repeats—until spools of repetition turn up in a laboratory.

The cutting room is a different landscape. There you sit, in a bright cubicle, with a stack of shallow cans of film at your elbow, a red china-pencil in your hand, your face bent to the viewer of the Movieola, where the film is passing, enlarged to the plainness of a snapshot. You stop the machine, run it backwards for a moment or two, send the sequence through again, and mark a suggested ending with your red pencil. You copy the number of feet counted by the meter. That is the end of a crucial sequence in a film. What has been done? And what is the audience going to see? For the externals of the studio do, in the end, have something to do with the finished film. But to speak of the externals of the cutting room is as if I were to say, about the writing of a poem: I sit at this table with the light held in the bottle of ink and glancing off the paper; I draw a sheet of white paper where my right hand may easily move on it and I lead the flow of ink across the page. Paper, ink, words are no more the material of poetry than the film, the marks on the sound track, the shears, are the material of movies. Yet they enter in. But the editor in the cutting room is dealing in time, in rhythms of length and relationship. As far as the making of films goes, when the functions are identified so that there is again—as in the modest documentaries, or in Chaplin's procedure—a writer-director-editor, some unity of imagination may appear in the finished work.

THE RELATIONSHIP OF IMAGES

For these sequences are thrown into relation with each other to make a movie. The selection and ordering are a work of preparation and equilibrium, of the breaking of the balance and the further growth. The single image, which arrives with its own speed, takes its place in a sequence which reinforces that image.

This happens most recognizably in films and in poetry. If you isolate certain moments in Hitchcock films, you have the illustration of the reinforced image that is used in poetry constantly. There was a point in *The Thirty-Nine Steps* at which a landlady opened the door of an apartment, walked in, and saw a corpse flung across the bed, with a knife handle rising fiercely from the dead back. The landlady turned to you, and opened her mouth with a scream of horror which was pure horror, and somehow more than a scream. The sound was not identified until a moment later, when you saw the train (carrying the hero away from the scene of the crime) as it hurled out of a black tunnel, still screaming, and you knew that the blast of its whistle had served for both voices.

Again, in *A Woman Alone* (which was shown under several names), there is a moment at the aquarium, when looking into a fish tank with two conspirators, safely meeting in this public and shadowy place, you see the water troubled by the motion of swimming, until a distortion is produced which makes the little streets and structures of the tank shudder and seem to lean.

Suddenly it is clear, not only that the bomb that these conspirators have plotted has gone off, and that this fish tank is Piccadilly Circus, and the walls are falling down; but also a comment on the nature of explosion is made clear. An explosion, says the image in the fish tank, is distortion, is maximum derangement from the human being's point of view, is a warping of reality that becomes more unbearable as you see it more clearly; in this case, as you see it more slowly. That comment is the reinforcement, the gift adding to our experience when an image is well-placed in a work of art which lives in time.

In the Russian film, *Life Is Beautiful*, the ending of war is shown in the form of earlier sequences *in reverse*: great explosions of earth are gathered back into the ground as you watch, melons push through the soil surface; in the ironic and moving quickness of wishful thinking.

In another Hitchcock film, *Foreign Correspondent*, one of the most exciting and melodramatic sequences ever made, the airplane crash in mid-ocean is accomplished with a minimum of reference, in the speed and economy of image that is to be found in concentrated poems. The only continuity is the screaming of the planes' engines in their fall. The first shot is one of the plane from outside; then the camera draws closer to the fuselage and we go in the window with it. From then on we are inside the plane, trapped in the fall. All we see are the fragmentary images of disaster: an end of the wing ripped; fear stamped on a face seen for a second; the posture of bodies braced in fall; the end of the wing breaking; the tense stubborn attitudes of the pilot and radio operator, staying at their posts at the more dangerous nose of the ship; the crowding of passengers towards the tail of the plane; the stump of wing; the water hurling into the cabin as the plane crashes in the sea. These are all fragments assembled; it is easy to reconstruct the way in which they were shot and joined; but we make the continuity in the theater. With one constant, the constant of sound,—and, threaded on that, a group of related but broken images, we make imaginatively an experience so satisfying and convincing and melodramatic that it is completely achieved within its own definition.

That definition does not expect very much. In *Alexander Nevsky,* the great scene of the battle on the ice; in *Paisan,* the great scenes in the marshes, slow and purposive and tragic in their risk; in *The Passion of Joan of Arc,* the turning of faces seen close; the stairs in *Potemkin;* these are all examples which have their parallels in poetry. In these sequences, the reinforcement of sensations or meanings—and in at least one of them, the aquarium scene, the comment on the nature of the event—lead to a revaluation.

But then interest to us as audience is not only in what we are seeing. The interest is fed by what we are doing. There is a pleasure in the assembling which, apart from all adult concerns, is the pleasure of the crucial moment of a young child at play when he makes a new arrangement of combinations and sees the possibilities of a new toy. That we call it "a toy" and "play" shows only the split in our later dealings with the world. Surely, in art, the distinction between work and play is again dissolved. The most interesting, here, is again where we do most, where (you would say of the child) "he plays the hardest."

The kind of engineering which allows us—leads us—to make the connections is inherent in movie-making as we know it, and it was accepted instantly, as far back as the shots of pounding hoofs in *The Birth of a Nation.* Our dreams, and all our experience, declare us animals who take pleasure in relating. The scientific material begins to arrive: the psychologists come to measure these responses, and the engineers in every field give us a tradition of form based on function and the preparation for function.

In art, there is no distinction between object and communication. The valid distinctions exist, and profusely. But they must be expressed in terms of the transfer between the artwork and the receiver, according to an experience which does not reject any part of the meaning. The intention of the artist, the methods—the bits of film on the cutting-room floor, the juggling of film sequences or the sections of a poem—these are technical considerations. When the practice of art is a base of our education, and when the search for truth in experience is regarded as something characteristic of the artist as well as the scientist, then the distinctions of judgment will be part of popular appreciation.

At this period, we see the converse of such possibility. Our schools do not now train the young to be artists; our movie studios now require writers who do not need to know how to write (according to Leo Rosten's Hollywood surveys); our culture as a whole does not produce an audience with belief in its own reactions. This is seen most clearly in the movie audience and the movie-makers. In Europe, there was always the idea of an aristocracy of intellectuals, taking its place of power among the other aristocracies; and this idea reaches us even through the younger and more venturesome publishers, who speak of building an elite of readers. We need never use such currency again, nor build a social structure of any kind in which the work of the group is directed towards the development of an elite. We have our symbols to build; but they are not to be the symbols of monarchies or elite groups. The symbols can be corrupted, the artists can be corrupted, the audience can be corrupted. Our history of movies shows that truth. But this, too, can be dealt with, and in one generation a new beginning can be made.

The writer becoming an employee in Hollywood, forced to conform to a code which dictates emotional limits, and producing material which can be censored and re-arranged, with or without his knowledge, is a key figure in our society. More than the political under orders, or the most constricted civil servant, he is the archetype of the citizen of the police state. It is not the state of which the satirists dream, with the dingy furnishings, the disconsolate weather, the sexless boredom, of anti-Utopia. The delight of strong sun and crashing rains and cool insinuating evenings, the attractive bodies and the green lights of custom, the drinks and the music and the money, are to be thought of along with the company-town aspect of a community which devotes itself to the *adjustment* of stories and ideas. Among all this, the political hunting, the robot extras, the technicians who never meet the "artists," the laid-off and rejected who live in the place, ready to be drawn on during a labor crisis of any kind; and the few working artists, dancing their razor-edge, pouring their energies into various fights: the fight to insist on their work's getting through, the fight to resist corruption of consciousness, the fight to organize the others.

A writer in Hollywood is expected to know how to make plot move along, and how to use colloquial dialogue. Of one hundred and thirty-five writers included in Rosten's survey, "only nine had experience in film editing, fifteen in direction, and less than five" (what can that mean?) "in sound."

The writer in Hollywood is used almost exactly as the writer in advertising is used. The middleman (the producer, the art director) has authority over him (and over the film director) and supposes himself to know more about the ways of expression and communication than the person who is expressing, who is communicating. The conference is the example of the breakdown of collective work: it is the farce of collective adjustment to a cynical ideal of the audience and the status quo. It is the burlesque of the psychiatrist's hope in a police state: to adjust to a corrupt idea of reality.

And if, in spite of every limitation, in spite of the twisted

imagination which changes the *ends* of stories, which shortens
the kiss, and baits the rebel, and must like any competitive business push the most expensive product hardest; in spite of the
slickness and thinness of almost any serious movie made here,
when seen with a first-rate French or Italian movie in which
human experience and passion provides a density of life
unmatched in American movies; in spite of the constant goad-
ing of a handful of reliable critics; there is a vitality here, a
practiced sureness like the sureness of an athlete. The athlete's
concentration is in the suspense of a good thriller; the teamwork
in the best of the flashy musicals is superb; and in the boldest
moments of these, the beating of your blood, the sensation of
cold at the temples, the drawing inside the mouth like the
moment after eating hot applesauce.

GOING TO THE MOVIES

What is it to us, to *go to the movies?*

It is the reconciliation with each other: this is what everybody
likes.

This is produced out of a multitude of constrictions. Think
what it might be, if there were only the true tension, between
the individual and his surroundings, in a kind of freedom, with
the rhythms given their full importance and with a primitive eye!

DOCUMENTARY AND SOME OTHER EXPERIMENTS

"It was forgotten," Paul Rotha writes, in *Documentary Film,*
"that their rhythms stood as symbols of an epoch and that there
is no real value in movement itself. They shot, these aesthetes,
the rhythms of a rotary press or the parade of a milk-bottling
machine and rested content with the visual effects of movement.
They did not, for a moment, realize that these repetitive rhythms,
beautiful to watch in themselves, raised important materialist

issues of the men at the machine, of the social and economic problems lying behind modern machinery and transport...."

This was printed ten years ago: by now, the commercial film has absorbed all the methods of the documentary. We have, in feature films, the half-documentary, the octoroon, the mulatto; not taking their places as the people do (with the exception of films like *Boomerang*), not advancing in their style, but using these methods as tricks. They were not tricks, the documentary methods that made a young art. They were functions of real information in real art. But we saw a curious thing happen within a decade, over the tops of such completely realized films as *Night Mail*, *China Strikes Back*, *The River*, *These Are the Men*. All of these films had flaws which were apparent. They were flaws, however, in a series of well-thought, honest, and creative ventures. There was a flaw in the young movement that has stopped it, temporarily at any rate, and allowed Hollywood to take over its methods to use well or as tricks. The flaw was this: that, working with a set of durable principles, the small groups making documentary films allowed themselves the luxury of feeling that the principles alone would hold. They did not go on creating. They did not even go on inventing. The youngest art, the art which could have been a revolutionary one, became the newest cliché.

But the documentary film, so precious to us during its early days, has left its clues. The combination of documentary with enacted film has been fertile. And the work of Joris Ivens, Paul Rotha, Grierson, Legge, Lerner, Steiner, Van Dyke, Strand, Hurwitz, Ferno, Kline, Flaherty, and the groups that formed behind such productions as *Spanish Earth*, *Crisis*, *Native Land*, *The City*, and *Heart of Spain* sent an impulse through the other arts. Not fully brave, their hesitations were crucial. They were not able to invent, finally, and they were not able to teach. The musicians associated with them: Aaron Copland, Hanns Eisler,

Virgil Thomson, Alex North, went on to commercial film music, theater music, and to their own work with a sharpening of the interactions in their music. The few writers associated with these filmmakers could use what they gained in everything they did. Auden, for example, has not gone on, except in theater forms, but the extremely fine Choruses of his early plays are nearer to film than the poems he wrote for such documentaries as *Night Mail*. Ben Maddow (David Wolff) in Hollywood, has used the fine combining of film methods in poems and a novel. I know that the writing for documentaries was confined by some of the limitations reflected from commercial movies. These experimenters hesitated before experiment.

The makers of "art" films, notably Cocteau and Prévert in France, Pudovkin, Dovzhenko, and Eisenstein in the Soviet Union, and the makers of *Grand Illusion, Kameradschaft, La Kermesse Héroique*, make their values come through, experiment, and survive. Rossellini and René Clair have entered from another way, and the flavors of these influences sharpen the best movies we know. The small daring comedies and documentaries, the heroic European full-length films, with their passion and development, have been criticized for being "slow" and "lyrical" by newspaper reviewers spoiled by high gloss and high speed and—for the most part—distractions instead of love, distractions instead of meaning, even distractions instead of sex. It is in our movies that we have achieved a narrative form where these cannot be allowed to carry, where the image may be prolonged, but the meaning must be cut short.

Our animated cartoons have been amazing creations of violence and fun, color, cruelty, and brilliant sound. Their drawing, however, has been frozen into one style: the style of Disney and the comic strip; we are cut off both from the marvelous intensities of Len Lye's design or the subtle movement and depth of air of Lotte Reiniger's silhouettes. Artists have dreamed of making animations of their own styles: Masereel made, or almost finished, one such film, and there are undoubtedly others, but this work needs a workshop and a lab, and only the enduring pioneers (like Lotte Reiniger, whose animations have not been shown here) have finished their films. If there were a project to allow artists, from Thurber and Price to Low and Grosz, to experiment with their own drawings; and then to invite the painters who might be interested in film to make the outlines for their animations, a limited field would again be opened up.

THE FREEING OF THE SOUND TRACK

In our feature films, our documentaries, our newsreels (which have become extremely important editorially), and our cartoons, one omission is apparent. This is an omission common to all the graphic arts which exist in combination. It meets us in the labels beneath the photographs in our picture magazines; in almost every kind of film, it comes through as the same lack. It is not only a weakness of the sound track. Its origin is deep in the conception of film. Its result is that both sound and silence are thrown away.

Perhaps the history of this weakness mirrors the history of film, in that the silent film preceded sound. I do not think so. Some of the silent movies used their captions well; many threw them away, showing a slide only when the producers were not sure that the pantomime was plain, or when they were afraid that they could not handle exposition.

But, in film as we know it now, the sound track has not been at all developed. I am not referring simply to a narrator's voice, the exposition of the action, the "voice" about which Pirandello used to talk to Eisenstein; or only to the dialogue, which has been for the most part brought over from notions of stage dialogue even when the image track is true film. I am thinking of the entire sound track in relation to the image and to the film as a whole.

The function of the person who works with the sound would be that of writer-musician. He would work with the creative use of sound as the great directors have worked with the composition and "framing" of their scenes. He would see the meaning of words and music and noise and silence as part of the dramatic unity of the film. Failures like the bad movies based on Shakespeare would mark his road, as well as the near-failures of other plays and of the "good" movies based on Shakespeare, remarkable because they are movies at all. For this example is the illuminating one: suppose we had a true film treatment of Shakespeare, using the capacities of film, from the inner monologue that has often been suggested, to the possibilities of montage and the voyages of the eye that were attempted as beginnings in Olivier's Shakespearean films?

Suppose that we had, above all, a freeing of the sound track.

The sound track, as far as the finished film is concerned, may be thought of as pasted to the image track. There is no reason why the juxtapositions that have been marvelous to us in the image track—and in poetry—should not be used in sound. We are slower with sound than with sight, and that physiological fact should also be used. But there is every reason to acknowledge the riches of sound in juxtaposition: the conversation, say, that sent this plane up, heard as the plane is seen; the plane's engine heard over the next meeting of the two men we saw were responsible. The depth of sound, in focus, is as moving as the depth of vision can be. Orson Welles, who is almost the only person to have made a beginning in these depths, has used sound creatively from time to time. A few of the animated cartoons have declared, in their way, their willingness. But the two methods of conceiving the flow of images—linkage and collision—may be applied to sound also.

LANGUAGE AND THE FLOW OF IMAGES

Language, in this sense, is a part of the sound track and a part of the image track.

There has been no work at all done with language in films. The history of film language is a history of essays in the collo-quial. False breaks into stilted stage dialogue are at one pole, and a synthetic vernacular at the other. When a master of language—Shaw or Cocteau—is present, the film reaches, not another dimension, but its true life in words. The speech of *Jane Eyre*, on whose script Aldous Huxley worked, was moving beyond anything that had been in the theater for a long time.

But indeed I am not speaking only of dialogue. The freeing of the image has been a process of intense beauty and interest. The freeing of the sound track means the bringing of poetry to the screen—not poetry in the formal historic sense, but a new appropriate poetry, now unborn. To understand the possibilities of language moving against, as well as with, a flow of images, will be to understand new values in film as well as in poetry. The combination of narrator, the voices of dialogue, music, sound, and beyond these voices from anywhere—as the images may be images from anywhere for which we are prepared—will give us a new function. We are the age to develop this function, and the film is a matrix for the new form.

To move through this door, however, will require a sense of revelation as well as a steady and human grasp of reality and meaning. The door itself is there. It is real.

AJANTA

In India, in the caves of Ajanta, generations of painter-monks left on the rocky walls a series of frescoes painted according to a method lost, after the sixth century A.D., to the Eastern world and never known in the West. The method was a religious one.

In our tradition of representational painting, the frame is a window; through it we see these landscapes, this room, these men and women under the lights we know. The canvas of the picture is denied, or rather a double attitude is taken. The painter, classically, draws figures on the plane of the picture—on the canvas; the beholder knows he is meant to look *through* the canvas at the painted scene. Cézanne paints solids, but we reach them beyond the canvas. The trickiest of the trompe l'oeil paintings disregard the plane entirely.

The school of Buddhist painter-monks at Ajanta believed a different principle. They felt that the sensation of space within ourselves is the analogy by which the world is known. The rocks of the cave walls were real; they emphasized their crystals and prisms; these boulders, it is said, have the energy of a locomotive on the screen. Painting is not to lead away from reality. Against the walls, for there is no background as we know, start the figures, the holy figures of the life of Buddha, dancing, taking their ease, moving against flowered lawns, palaces, processions, the carnal scenes of the world. Everything is bathed in light; there is no shadow cast. There is no distortion except for movement and meaning: this red cow is elongated, neck, back, and flanks, for she is running.

There is a web of movement, in which these pillars, like candles, are coordinates. The Western idea of still life is unknown. There is no still life, there is life, and all life shares the movement of the mind. In living reality, all is movement. This is the dance, and it is to be acknowledged in art.

"No object is isolated," Kramrisch says of the Ajanta paintings. Each is carried by its origin. They are strung together by their rhythm; they yield themselves to the connections.

Here are you, in the cave. The walls are real, and they are accepted. You are confronted by the figures of your consciousness. They start out of the real walls, filling the space of the cave.

In this life, in this living contemplation, there is no sound. To it its language may be brought.

Our experience, set in our time in the world, may be shared through any art. We are ready for the pictures of our true life, we are ready for the poems of our true life.

All the forms wait for their full language. The poems of the next moment are at hand.

Art is not in the world to deny any reality. You stand in the cave, the walls are on every side. The walls are real. But in the space between you and the walls, the images of everything you know, full of fire and possibility, life appearing as personal grace, says Kramrisch. Dancing: creating, destroying, taking possession.

There is here a reciprocal reality. It is the clue to art; and it needs its poetry.

PART FOUR

⌒

THE LIFE
OF POETRY

⊙

CHAPTER TEN

THE RARE UNION: POETRY AND SCIENCE

In time of the crises of the spirit, we are aware of all of need, our need for each other and our need for ourselves. We call up our fullness; we turn, and act. We begin to be aware of correspondences, of the acknowledgment in us of necessity, and of the lands.

And poetry, among all this—where is there a place for poetry?

If poetry as it comes to us through action were all we had, it would be very much. For the dense and crucial moments, spoken under the stress of realization, full-bodied and compelling in their imagery, arrive with music, with our many kinds of theater, and in the great prose. If we had these only, we would be open to the same influences, however diluted and applied. For these ways in which poetry reaches past the barriers set up by our culture, reaching toward those who refuse it in essential presence, are various, many-meaning, and certainly—in this period—more acceptable. They stand in the same relation to poetry as applied science to pure science.

If there were no poetry on any day in the world, poetry would be invented that day. For there would be an intolerable hunger. And from that need, from the relationships within ourselves and among ourselves as we went on living, and from every other expression of man's nature, poetry would be—I cannot here say invented or discovered—poetry would be derived. As research science would be derived, if the energies we now begin to know reduced us to a few people, rubbing into life a little fire.

However, there is this poetry. There is this science. The farther along the way we go in each, the more clearly the relationship may be perceived, the more prodigal the gifts.

The definitions of Western culture have, classically, separated these two disciplines. When Darwin wrote of Humboldt that he displayed the rare union between poetry and science, he set the man in a line of heroes of that meeting-place—a line which includes Lucretius and Goethe and Leonardo, but which for the last centuries has been obscured in the critical structure which insists that the forms of imagination are not only separate, but exclusive.

The scientist has suffered before the general impoverishment of imagination in some of the same ways as the poet. The worker in applied science and the inventor might be thought of as the town crackpots, but there was always the reservation of an audience, like children lined up before a holiday conjuror, waiting to be shown. The theoretical scientist, like the poet, could never "show" his audience: they lacked language, and in another way, so did he. Unless the law could be translated into an image, it kept the pure scientist in a position remote from his society. He would be called "abstract," "obscure": he would be a freak of intellect, even to the members of his house.

The explosion of a bomb ended that period. The function of science was declared, loudly enough for the unborn to hear. The test on the bombing range at Alamogordo proved one series of devoted researches; Hiroshima, Nagasaki, Bikini, Eniwetok, acted out others. Only the human meanings were left to explore: the power for life.

That dramatizing of poetry, in a shock of annunciation, can never take place. For poetry is, at every instant, concerned with meaning. The poet—of the kind of poetry for which I hope— knows that consciousness and creation are linked, and cannot be postponed. The scientist of the science I hope for knows that too. And more than this recognition is shared, even in our flawed reality. The union Darwin named is true.

Kronecker said of mathematicians, "We are all poets!" The remark provoked assent and sneers; it was noticed.

To believe any of these statements, one must believe, with Clerk Maxwell, that science must turn to the "singular point" and the unique; in a structure of probabilities, he must hunt out the improbable. The conventional scientist, schoolbound, disavows everything but measurement and classification; he breaks his science into countries; he excludes what he considers inexact. He becomes more and more the reactionary, working for a uniform world. The dogma is one of repetition; a ritual nonsense is uttered, in a loud voice; and suitable tests for the conforming of other scientists and the rest of the citizenry are performed by these, who—working scientists, educators, politicians, critics of all forms—now will swear they are behaving scientifically.

William James met one such, in the person of a lady from Boston. As F. O. Matthiessen tells it, James was presenting one of his lucid, cogent arguments, and paused to say ironically, "That is like asking 'What holds the world up?'" The lady from Boston, impatient with all the talk, answered with clipped decision, "A rock." James wanted to take this farther—"What holds the rock up?" he asked. The lady said, "Another rock." "And *that* rock," James pursued, "what holds *it* up?" The lady stiffened. "Young man," she said in a voice that a dog-hater might use on an off-bounds Pekinese, "let me make myself clear: it's rocks, all the way!"

The dogma and shrinking from the external world are at one limit of the range of belief. At the other are science and poetry and, indeed, reality.

Correspondences between the two are many. Art and science have instigated each other from the beginning; sparsely when the conclusions, the answers, were translated from one form to the other; always more fruitfully when the questions were used. This is surely because the answers are distinct, and because both science and poetry are languages ready to be betrayed in translation; but their roots spread through our tissue, their deepest meanings fertilize us, and reaching our consciousness, they reach each other.

They make a meeting-place. There are opposites here; identity is not Aristotelian; it is rather the identity of Whitman and of modern science. But it includes a unity.

THE UNITY OF IMAGINATION

George Sarton writes, in his *History of Science*, of the unity of nature, which is offered in every new law's discovery, and in the independent determining of every constant. The history of science, clearly showing the interdependence of the sciences, and often presenting simultaneous discoveries, leads him to conclude that science is one. The blind collaboration, of people of many nations, in discovery, declares to him the unity of mankind.

"It is hardly necessary to enlarge on this," he adds in his candid and revealing Introduction, "or to show that these three unities—the unity of nature, the unity of science, and the unity of mankind—are but three different visages of the same unity. In all probability there are still other aspects, though less obvious and less certain, for example, the unity of art and the unity of religion."

He speaks of his work, which illustrates the fundamental unity. "And this helps us to understand the real significance of human progress; it is the gradual transformation of that potential or hidden unity into an actual unity, one that all can see and no one deny."

That statement, it seems to me, is one of the clearest declarations of the gift of this age: the secular announcement of a possibility which had before reached men and women only through their religions, implemented with exclusions. These exclusions are not fundamental to the faith, but to the temporal power of any organized church: rooted in defense, fed on persecution, they have become the living stockade around every orthodox religious grouping.

But our age, in the promise of its science and its poetry, has made available to all people the idea of one world. The million suffering, the wars of the past, the false barriers, offer whatever good survived to that simple idea, the old idea and seed of hope which has never died except to grow. The religious ideas, of which this is one, strike with the impact of simplicity, carried to its limits, and immediately understandable. Contained in this truth is the belief in the unity of imagination.

A REMARK BY BAUDELAIRE

When Baudelaire said that the imagination is "the most scientific of the faculties, because it alone understands the universal analogy," he set the trap and sprung it in one phrase. The trap is the use of the discoveries of science instead of the methods of science. Woodrow Wilson was caught there, when he called for a Darwinian, rather than Newtonian, system of government.

The coherence of one kind of discovery is not the coherence of another. We recognize constantly; but in that recognition, we are lost unless we realize that there is little uniformity.

The biased abstraction which is all experience as well as all classification (in D. L. Watson's phrase) carries us to the creative process. And here Baudelaire does spring his trap, for the analogy is *universal*. Imagination finds, and combines, to make its works more human. Knowledge and effective action are met here, too, in one gesture; the gesture of understanding the world and changing it.

Sometimes the conclusions meet, and we prove each other. I remember a visit that Charles Biederman, the "abstract" artist in metals and plastics and concrete, made to the early work in Chicago on the cyclotron. Biederman was shown through by a friend of his, a scientist who out of courtesy asked him what he thought of the structural design. The scientist expected an uncritical answer, and was startled into rudeness when the artist said, "It would be *very good*, according to my standards, except for one thing: that joint—if you put a sphere in, just there, it could really be called perfect." On his next visit, months later, he met the scientist who said, "Do you remember what I called you, last time? Well, you'd better know what's happened. Things kept going wrong, and the trouble was traced to just that joint. They put a sphere in; everything's smooth now."

One of the most fully realized connections between the forms of imagination was made in the writing of Henry Adams, who entered the century consciously, having absorbed the relationships he would need as working instruments. He brought the definitions of unity and multiplicity to Chartres, to the work of Gibbs, to the discovery of radium, and to political history the image which he predicted would be the crucial one for our period: the image of the bomb. Writing of science and the rush of phase, he found himself—with Melville in his way, with Jeffers in his—cold and lost before annihilation. The languages are not the same: for one it is the devouring of evil and the sea, for one the black crystals of inhuman space and inhuman destruction, for one the heat-death, entropy. But they consider annihilation.

From where do the answers come? The next answers, that must come in the form of questions?

We know what Galileo muttered. What is our *E pur si muove*?

Is there a clue in the idea of the unity of imagination, the meeting-place between science and poetry and between one man and another?

THE LIFE OF THE SYMBOLS

Science is a system of relations.

Poincaré, saying so, says also, "It is before all a classification, a manner of bringing together facts which appearances separate, though they are bound together by some natural and hidden kinship....

"It is in the relations alone that objectivity must be sought; it would be vain to seek it in beings considered as isolated from one another....

"External objects...for which the word *object* was invented, are really *objects* and not fleeting and fugitive appearances, because they are not only groups of sensations, but groups cemented by a constant bond. It is this bond, and this bond alone, which is the object in itself, and this bond is a relation.

"Therefore, when we ask what is the objective value of science, that does not mean: Does science teach us the true nature of things? but it means: Does it teach us the true relations of things?"

The search of man is a long process toward this reality, the reality of the relationships. One meaning of that search is love; one meaning is progress; one is science; and one is poetry.

For there is no human level on which the search does not exist. It may be objected, here, that the whole notion is a mirror of the mind. It is that; and of the emotions, too; of one situation regarding ourselves and each other; it is the expression which a total response to any experience evokes.

In science, the relationships may be expressed symbolically, using symbols designed for specific work.

The use of language involves symbols so general, so dense emotionally, that the life of the symbols themselves must continually be taken into consideration. In poetry, the relations are not formed like crystals on a lattice of words, although the old criticism (which at the moment is being called, of course, the New Criticism) would have us believe it so. Poetry is to be regarded according to a very different set of laws. I hope shortly to offer you a preliminary suggestion of these.

A long work is now being devoted to research based on the conviction that "poetry is words"; research that is of value in classifying according to one theory of criticism. That theory is fashionable now, I believe; and fashions in words are interesting to know. I have a high regard for some of the poets who are setting up these structures: dissecting poetry into ideas and things, and letting the life escape; or counting words as they might count the cells of a body; or setting the "impression" against the "scientific truth" in order to dismiss them both. But I cannot accept what they say. It seems to me that something is dragging at their words. They seem to be ignoring the most apparent facts of our condition in this period. What produces this sense of drag? These are cultivated people; yet, in all of their statements, one evidence after another shows that they are thinking in terms of static mechanics. Their treatment of language gives away their habit of expecting units (words, images, arguments) in which, originating from certain premises, the conclusion is inevitable. The treatment of correspondence (metaphor, analogy) is always that of a two-part equilibrium in which the parts are self-contained.

When Emerson said that language was fossil poetry, he was leading up to some of these contemporary verdicts. If we can think of language as it is, as we use it—as a process, in which

motion and relationship are always present—as a river in whose
watercourse the old poetry and old science are both continually
as countless pebbles and stones and boulders rolled, recognized
in their effect on the color and the currents of the stream—we
will be closer. To think of language as earth containing fossils
immediately sets the mind, directs it to rigid consequences. The
critics of the "New" group, going on from there, see poetry itself
as fossil poetry. It will simplify the amending of these ideas—
which tend with more and more of a list of error toward a
wretched and static condition, to which nothing is appropriate
but anguish and forgiveness—if we dismiss every static pro-
nouncement and every verdict which treats poetry as static.

THE ARRANGEMENT IS THE LIFE

Truth is, according to Gibbs, not a stream that flows from a
source, but an agreement of components. In a poem, these
components are, not the words or images, but the relations
between the words and images. Truth is an accord that actually
makes the whole "simpler than its parts"; as he was fond of saying. Originality is important before the accord is reached; it is
the most vivid of the means in a poem, and the daring of the
images allows the reader to put off his emotional burden of association with the single words, allows him to come fresh to
memory and to discovery. But when the whole poem has taken
its effect—even its first effect—then the originality is absorbed
into a sense of order, and order then becomes the important factor. All of these words were known, as the results leading to a
scientific discovery may have been known. But they were not
arranged before the poet seized them and discovered their pattern. This arrangement turns them into a new poem, a new
science. Here, as everywhere, the arrangement is the life.

The arrangement, which is the life of a poem, includes music and meaning, the immediately experienced and the relations of ideas. The process of arrangement, or creation, is an essential and subtle one.

MESSAGE AND IMAGE: DANTE

Two descriptions of this activity may be compared here. F. S. C. Northrop, in an essay "The Functions and Future of Poetry," tells how Dante had read Saint Thomas Aquinas, whose *Summa* articulated the Church and Aristotle, and was inaccessible to the public of that period. Dante, according to this account, solved the problem of the period by "epistemically correlating" his own vivid response with "technical concepts" of the *Summa*. "Then he moved the images about" so that his poem conveyed the doctrine metaphorically. Northrop concludes that Dante in his "pure poetry" has immortality, but Dante as the conveyor of a theory belonging to the Middle Ages is dated; for us, "this poem has lost its message." Then, oddly, Northrop goes on to recommend that the poet of the future "take the new conception of the theoretic component of reality"—that is, contemporary symbolic logic and scientific philosophy—and present it in the fresh and moving terms which the poet can provide. The poet who can do this can "command the poetry and perhaps, in major part at least, even the culture of the future." Professor Northrop's work on the meeting of cultures has been extremely suggestive; there is a great deal in this essay that I question. As part of his analysis of the creative process, he makes it harshly clear that the poet is never to try to determine the truth of the doctrine—someone else's doctrine—which he is using. It is because poets do not have this capacity, he declares, that poetry is an art, rather than a science! The ideas I question here are 1) "Then he moved the images about"; 2) the robot poet putting a dominant philosophy into vivid language without caring about its truth (and what makes the poet appear to choose the philosophy? and what makes language vivid?); and 3) the bit about "commanding" the "culture" of the future.

THE MOTION OF IMAGES

The creation of a poem, or mathematical creation, involves so much sense of arrival, so much selection, so much of the desire that makes choice—even though one or more of these may operate in the unconscious or partly conscious work periods before the actual work is achieved—that the questions raised are very pertinent. I rely for my information about mathematical creation on such sources as Poincaré, who speaks of the mind seeming to act only of itself and on itself, selecting, making only the useful combinations, choosing, and finally being struck, as by strong light, with certainty. The poet chooses and selects and has that sense of arrival as the poem ends; he is expressing what it feels like to arrive at his meanings. If he has expressed that well, his reader will arrive at his meanings. The degree of appropriateness of expression depends on the preparing. By preparing I mean allowing the reader to feel the interdependences, the relations, within the poem.

These inter-dependences may be proved, if you will allow the term, in one or more ways: the music by which the syllables resolve may lead to a new theme, as in a verbal music, or to a climax, a key-relationship which makes—for the moment—an equilibrium; the images may have established their own progression in such a way that they serve to mark the poem's development; the tensions and attractions between the poem's meanings may mark its growth, as they must if the poem is to achieve its form.

A poem is an imaginary work, living in time, indicated in language. It is and it expresses; it allows us to express.

The fact that it extends in time means that motion is internal to the poem.

An image in a poem is not at all like an image in a painting. Even if the poem is so short that the time spent in reading it will hardly send the sweep-second hand around, it has moved through its sequences and exists in a time-relation; the images have each been set in motion, so that they carry throughout, reverberating backward and forward, influencing all the other images. And so for the sounds: The first *s* and *st* and *th* and *t* of these lines—watch them, listen to them as they carry forward in

> *...that sustaining love*
> *Which through the web of being blindly wove*
> *By man and beast and earth and air and sea*
> *Burns bright or dim, as each are mirrors of*
> *The fire for which all thirst.*

Everyone has always recognized, I began to say, that motion is inherent in poetry and music. Lucretius wrote, "moving the sleeping images of things toward the light," and Percival

> *of all who bear*
> *Their forms in motion, when the spirit tends*
> *Instinctive, in their common good to share....*

and the phrase "current of thought" is in the language. There are countless examples, in the poets' and in conversation's metaphor.

But the meaning that this basic truth has for the laws of poetry has not pursued the knowledge of it. If you consider the pleasure with which we may read the finest writers of our own period on poetry, the graceful and dignified formal passages will return to you; they are said to be our glories. These discussions of Milton and Hopkins, Herbert, Auden, Yeats. But the motion of the poem does not enter: the talk is in terms of the start, the image, the crystallization. The passion, the intensity in form, of a great poem, are not here. They do not stand: they fly through, and over. The luck of the book is that we then may go back, to the top of the page, and begin to arrive again.

FORM, TIME, TENSION

The form of a poem is much more organic, closer to other organic form, than has been supposed. D'Arcy Wentworth Thompson, whose book *On Growth and Form* is a source and a monument, says that organic form is, mathematically, a function of time. There is, in the growth of a tree, the story of those years which saw the rings being made: between those wooden rippled rings, we can read the wetness or dryness of the years before the charts were kept. But the tree is in itself an image of adjustment to its surroundings. There are many kinds of growth: the inorganic shell or horn presents its past and present in the spiral; the crocus grows through minute pulsations, each at an interval of twenty seconds or so, each followed by a partial recoil.

A poem moves through its sounds set in motion, and the reaction to these sounds, their rhymes and repetitions and contrast, has a demonstrable physical basis which can be traced as the wavelength of the sounds themselves can be traced. The wavelength is measurable; the reaction, if you wish such measurements, could be traced through heartbeat and breath, although I myself do not place much value on such measurement.

The impact of the images, and the tension and attraction between meanings, these are the clues to the flow of contemporary poetry. Baudelaire, Lawrence, Eliot have been masters here, and well have known the effects and the essences they offered. But to go on, to recognize the energies that are transferred between people when a poem is given and taken, to know the relationships in modern life that can make the next step, to see the tendencies in science which can indicate it, that is for the new poets.

In the exchange, the human energy that is transferred is to be considered.

THE EXCHANGE

Exchange is creation; and the human energy involved is consciousness, the capacity to produce change from the existing conditions.

Into the present is flung naked life. Life is flung into the present language. The new forms emerge, with their intensive properties, or potentials—their words and images; and their extensive properties, existing in time: sound, forms, subjects, content, and that last includes all the relations between the words and images of the poem.

When the poem arrives with the impact of crucial experience, when it becomes one of the turnings which we living may at any moment approach and enter, then we become more of our age and more primitive. Not primitive as the aesthetes have used the term, but complicated, fresh, full of dark meaning, insisting on discovery, as the experience of a woman giving birth to a child is primitive.

I cannot say what poetry is; I know that our sufferings and our concentrated joy, our states of plunging far and dark and turning to come back to the world—so that the moment of intense turning seems still and universal—all are here, in a music like the music of our time, like the hero and like the anonymous forgotten; and there is an exchange here in which our lives are met, and created.

CHAPTER ELEVEN

A LIGHTNING FLASH

Exchange is creation.

In poetry, the exchange is one of energy. Human energy is transferred, and from the poem it reaches the reader. Human energy, which is consciousness, the capacity to produce change in existing conditions.

But the manner of exchange, the gift that is offered and received—these must be seen according to their own nature.

Fenollosa, writing of the Chinese written character as a medium for poetry, says this: "All truth is the transference of power. The type of sentence in nature is a flash of lightning. It passes between two terms, a cloud and the earth."

This is the threshold, now the symbols are themselves in motion. Now we have the charge, flaming along the path from its reservoir to the receptive target. Even that is not enough to describe the movement of reaching a work of art.

One of our difficulties is that, accepting a science that was static and seeing the world about us according to the vision it afforded, we have tried to freeze everything, including living functions, and the motions of the imaginative arts.

We have used the term "mind" and allowed ourselves to be

trapped into believing there was such a *thing*, such a *place*, such a locus of forces. We have used the word "poem" and now the people who live by division quarrel about "the poem as object." They pull it away from their own lives, from the life of the poet, and they attempt to pull it away from its meaning, from itself; finally, in a trance of shattering, they deny qualities and forms and all significance. Then, cut off from its life, they see the dead Beauty: they know what remorse is, they begin to look for some single cause of their self-hatred and contempt. There is, of course, no single cause. We are not so mechanical as that. But there was a symptom: these specialists in dying, they were prepared to believe there was such a thing as Still Life. For all things change in time; some are made of change itself, and the poem is of these. It is not an object; the poem is a process.

POET, POEM, AND WITNESS

Charles Peirce takes Fenollosa's lightning flash, sets it away from the giving. Peirce writes: "All dynamical action, or action of brute force, physical or psychical, either takes place between two subjects...or at any rate is a resultant of such actions between pairs." It is important here to understand what Peirce means by *semiosis*. By semiosis I mean, on the contrary, an action, or influence, which is, or involves, a cooperation of *three* subjects, such as a sign, its object, and its interpretant; this tri-relative influence not being in any way resolvable into actions between pairs...."

The giving and taking of a poem is, then, a triadic relation. It can never be reduced to a pair: we are always confronted by the poet, the poem, and the audience.

The poet, at the moment of his life at which he finished the poem.

The poem, as it is available, heard once, or in a book always at hand.

The audience, the individual reader or listener, with all his life, and whatever capacity he has to summon up his life appropriately to receive more life. At this point, I should like to use another word: "audience" or "reader" or "listener" seems inadequate. I suggest the old word "witness," which includes the act of seeing or knowing by personal experience, as well as the act of giving evidence. The overtone of responsibility in this word is not present in the others; and the tension of the law makes a climate here which is that climate of excitement and revelation giving air to the work of art, announcing with the poem that we are about to change, that work is being done on the self.

These three terms of relationship—poet, poem, and witness—are none of them static. We are changing, living beings, experiencing the inner change of poetry.

The relationships are the meanings, and we have very few of the words for them. Even our tests, the personality tests of which we presently are so proud, present the static forms of Rohrschach blotches. Any change must be seen as specifically in the examinee. Tests are to be made for the perception of change. We need tests in time, moving images on film, moving sounds and syllables on records; or both on sound film. Then we could begin to see how changing beings react to changing signs—how the witness receives the poem.

In a test of recognition, hardly a person knew his own hands, or his face in profile, or his body from behind. It was only when the group was shown films in which they could see themselves walking—face blanked out—that empathy arrived, and with it, recognition.

We know our own rhythms. Our rhythms are more recognizably our selves than any of our forms. Sometimes in nature, form and rhythm are very close: the shape of a tree, for example, is the diagram of its relation to every force which has acted on it and in it; the "shape" of our consciousness—but you see to what folly use of models may lead.

The laws of exchange of consciousness are only suspected. Einstein says, "Now I believe that events in nature are controlled by a much stricter and more closely binding law than we recognize today, when we speak of one event being the *cause* of another. We are like a child who judges a poem by the rhymes and knows nothing of the rhythmic pattern. Or we are like a juvenile learner at the piano, *just* relating one note to that which immediately precedes or follows. To an extent this may be very well when one is dealing with very simple and primitive compositions; but it will not do for an interpretation of a Bach fugue."

I believe that one suggestion of such law is to be found in the process of poetry.

It is the process and the arrangement that give us our clues. Here the links between the scientist and the poet are strong and apparent.

The links between poetry and science are a different matter. For, in recent poetry, there is to be seen a repetition of old fallacies. The by-products, the half-understood findings of science have been taken over, with the results of tragedy.

You may see these results in fashionable poetry: in the poetry of the sense of annihilation, of the smallness of things, of aversion, guilt, and the compulsion toward forgiveness. This is strong magic here: if they want smallness, they will have their smallness; if they want it, they will at last have their forgiveness. But these artists go blaming, blaming. Let us look at what has happened. With the exploration of time and the newer notions of the universe, we have a generation who half-read the findings as they are popularized, and who emerge with little but self-pity. A characteristic title is The World Has Shrunk in the Wash.

What has really happened? What does this "smallness" mean to us?

It means that in ourselves we go on from the world of primitive man, a "small" world surrounded by the unknown—whether that unknown be the jungle or curved infinity. Again, the "large" things are human capacities and the beliefs they live among. Our relation to each other and to ourselves are the only things with survival value, once again. We can go on from a source in ourselves which we had almost lost. We can go on with almost forgotten strengths which are—according to your bias—profoundly religious, profoundly human. We can understand the primitive—not as the clumsy, groping naif of a corrupted definition, or even the unskilled "unsophisticate" of modern aesthetic usage—for what he was and what we have to be: the newborn of an age, the pioneer, Adam who dares.

The century has only half-prepared us to be primitives. The time requires our full consciousness, humble, audacious, clear; but we have nightmares of contradiction. For all its symptoms of liberation, its revolutionary stirrings in persons and peoples, the Victorian period was also one of swollen dreams. Behind us overhang the projections of giantism, the inflated powers over all things, according to which nature became some colony of imperial and scientific man, and Fact and Logic his throne and sceptre. He forgot that that sceptre and that throne were signs. Fact is a symbol, Logic is a symbol: they are symbols of the real.

THE COMPLETION OF EXPERIENCE

And reality may be seen as the completion of experience.

Experience itself cannot be seen as a point in time, a fact. The experience with which we deal, in speaking of art and human growth, is not only the event, but the event *and the entire past of the individual.* There is a series in any event, and the definition of the event is the last unit of the series. You read the poem: the poem you now have, the poem that exists in your imagination, is the poem and all the past to which you refer it.

The poet, by the same token, is the man (is the woman) with all the poet's past life, at the moment the poem is finished; that is, at the moment of reaching a conclusion, of understanding further what it means to feel these relationships.

A POETRY WORKSHOP

In reading poems with groups of people, doing what is called "teaching poetry," I have found that I can best proceed if I can offer an experience first. You may know the startling and loosening effect of being shown a blank piece of paper, with its properties and possibilities, and then of seeing it suddenly crumpled in the outstretched hand, to become something else, with its present properties and possibilities.

In a sheet of paper is contained the Infinite, wrote Lu Chi, in his *Essay on Literature* (300 A.D.—translated by Shih-Hsiang Chen)—and from Lu Chi to I. A. Richards, the power of space waiting to be filled is demonstrated. I have seen it in a classroom of people widely disparate in background and intention—ranging from shipyard workers and machinists to college and high-school students; newspaper people, from the Hearst paper and the left-wing paper; several housewives; a social worker, a poetry teacher, a Jungian analyst; a few office workers, a German avant-garde writer now working as an upholsterer; the tormented editor of a shipyard paper, another teacher, a draftsman, a dancer. There was a moment of challenge and shock, then some embarrassed blankness. Then they began, as any group begins, in response to this, to write: direct, subjective writing. When they read their pages to each other, they are well introduced. But this is prologue.

In workshops, it is possible to deal with the poems submitted at each meeting: the therapy of the poetry class which emphasizes personality does not apply. There is a power for health in the art workshop, but it functions best when there is writing being done as freely and as continually as possible, and when definite actions of reference are offered to the group.

The action which is closest to the nature of a poem is that which will dramatize the process of reaching a conclusion. I have called for a volunteer in workshop, and asked the intrepid one whether he could make a poem—quality set aside for the moment—on the spot. After his moment of blankness, we could see his face change, and soon he said he had something. I asked him whether he could remember it; and he said, Yes, he could. Then I asked him to leave the room, to wait in the hall and after a while, to write the poem down; I would come out for him a little later.

When he left the room, there was a stir. I asked the group whether there was a poem; with a few dissenters at first, they agreed that there was. Where did the poem exist? There was some discussion here; one angry person said the poem did not exist until it was on paper; the rest said it existed in the poet's mind, in the poet's imagination.

What was the poem made of, what was its material? I listed the answers on the blackboard. Sensations, impressions, ideals, response to immediate stimuli, memory, rhythm, rhyme, divine light, inspiration—what was it made of?—words, images, sounds. A few people hazarded guesses based on their assumptions of the bias of the volunteer—his poem would mean this, it would have that social content, its structure might be such—

I went out into the hall, where the volunteer waited with a slip of paper in his hand. Briefly, I told him what had happened in the room since he left.

He came back to his place, and read his poem. Yes, it was exactly as he had composed it, while we watched. Well, perhaps one word was different.

Would he tear up the slip of paper? He tore it into small bits, a little random heap on the table before him.

Now where was the poem?

At this point the discussion takes a new direction and impetus. The poem exists in the imagination of the poet and the group; but are there as many poems as there are witnesses? What is the role of the words on the paper? Even, as a professor at the University of California asked, what would have happened if the volunteer had died in the hall—would there have been a poem?

We are on the way to answers. The nature of this reality has been established. We have all *gone through* an experience to which the questions and answers may now refer. We have seen the difference between art—which is not destroyed when the paper is torn, because its material is not print on paper, but the imagination of the artist and the witnesses—and craft, whose material is otherwise. We have seen something come into existence, and be diffused—and, incidentally, we have seen how mistaken were the prejudices of the group concerning the prejudices of the poet. More has been acted out about point of view than a dozen lectures could describe—the difficult matter of the individual attitude, an "original relation to the universe," so elusive to the emotionally insecure, elusive to the point that one sometimes longs for the omission of the grammatical subject, as in classical Chinese writing—so that Shih-Hsiang Chen, in his comments on translation, says that he has translated the subject as "the poet," in an attempt to offer an expression "more connotative of a universal, objective viewpoint than 'I' or 'he.'" More has been acted out, in this workshop experiment, about the creative process, than any exposition could declare.

The process of writing a poem represents work done on the self of the poet, in order to make form. That this form has to do with the relationships of sounds, rhythms, imaginative beliefs does not isolate the process from any other creation. A total imaginative response is involved, and the first gestures of offering—even if the offering is never completed, and indeed even if the poem falls short. If it does, it has fallen in the conception, for the conception and the execution are identified here—whatever is conceived *is* made, is written.

Essentials are here, as in mathematical or musical creation—we need no longer distinguish, for we are speaking of the process itself, except for our illustrations. Only the essential is true; Joseph Conrad, in a letter of advice, drives this home by recommending deletions, explaining that these words are "not essential and therefore not true to the fact."

The process has very much unconscious work in it. The conscious process varies: my own experience is that the work on a poem "surfaces" several times, with new submergence after each rising. The "idea" for the poem, which may come as an image thrown against memory, as a sound of words that sets off a traveling of sound and meaning, as a curve of emotion (a form) plotted by certain crises of events or image or sound, or as a title which evokes a sense of inner relations; this is the first "surfacing" of the poem. Then a period of stillness may follow. The second surfacing may find the poem filled in, its voices distinct, its identity apparent, and another deep dive to its own depth of sleep and waiting. A last surfacing may find you ready to write. You may have jotted down a course of images, or a first line, or a whole verse, by now. This last conscious period finds you with all the work on yourself done—at least this is typical of the way I write a fairly sustained poem—and ready for the last step of all, the writing of the poem. Then the experience is followed, you reach its conclusion with the last word of your poem. One role is accomplished. At this point, you change into the witness. You remember what you may, and much or little critical work—re-writing—may be done.

I know most clearly the process of writing a recent, fairly extended poem, "Orpheus" [The Centaur Press, San Francisco, 1949]. The beginnings go far back, to childhood and a wish for identity, as rebirth, as coordination, as form. My interests here are double: a desire for form, and perhaps a stronger desire to understand the wish for form. The figure of Orpheus stands for loss and triumph over loss, among other things: the godhead of music and poetry, yes, in a mythology I was always familiar with at a distance at which it could be better dealt with than the mythology, say, of the Old Testament. In a poem written when I was nineteen, after a long hospitalization for typhoid fever contracted in an Alabama station house during the second Scottsboro trial—a poem called "In Hades, Orpheus," I focussed on Eurydice, the ill woman who yearns backward from the burning green of the world to the paleness and rest—and death—of the hospital. Then the interest in Orpheus himself took precedence: I was at the brilliant performance of Gluck's *Orpheus* which Tchelitchew designed for the Metropolitan Opera, and was moved by that play of loss and the dragging loves and the music and thorny volcanic Hell; so moved and disturbed that, years later, I wished to go on from there, not to revisit those scenes of Hell.

On Forty-Second Street, late one night, I saw the night-walkers go past the fifth-run movie houses, the Marine Bar, the Flea Circus, not as whole people, but as a leg, part of a shoulder, an eye askew. Pieces of people. This went into notes for a poem that never was written. They say "MARINE BAR, portraits of an eye and the mouth, blue leg and half a face." This was eight years before the poem was written. Then there was a period of writing other poems and prose, of being away from New York and returning, and then a time of great scattering, a year later, when I wrote what became the beginning of "The Antagonists":

> *Pieces of animals, pieces of all my friends*
> *prepare assassinations while I sleep...*

This was a poem that began with the tearing of the "I" and moved on to a reconciliation in love and intensity. Near the phrases, in my notebook, I wrote "bringing the dead back to life."

Four years later, reading Thomson and Geddes' *Life*, I became interested again in morphology and specifically in the fact that no part of the body lives or dies to itself. I read what I could about the memory and lack of memory of fragments, of amputees, and of dislocated nerve centers. And at the same time I was writing, as part of another poem,

> *Orpheus in hell remembered rivers*
> *and a music rose*
> *full of all human voices;*
> *all words you wish are in that living sound*
> *and even torn to pieces*
> *one piece sang*
> *Come all ye torn and wounded here*
> *together*
> *and one sang to its brother*
> *remembering.*

There, in Carmel, the course of the poem suddenly became clear. It did not concern Eurydice—not directly—it was of a later time. The murder of Orpheus began it; that early unsolved murder. Why did the women kill him? Reinach has written a paper about the murder. Was it because he loved Eurydice and would not approach them? Was it because he was homosexual, and they were losing their lovers to him? Was it because he had seen their orgies without taking part? All these theories had been advanced. But my poem started a moment later. I had it now! "Pieces of Orpheus," I wrote: that would be the title. The scene is the mountaintop, just after the murder. The hacked pieces lie in their blood, the women are running down the slope, there is only the mountain, the moon, the river, the cloud. He was able to make all things sing. Now they begin: "the voice of the Cloud to the killers of Orpheus," I wrote. I knew what would follow. The pieces of the body would begin to talk, each according to its own nature, but they would be lost, they would be nothing, being no longer together. Like those in love, apart, I thought. No, not like anything. Like pieces of the body, knowing there had been pain, but not able to remember what pain—knowing they had loved, but not remembering whom. They know there must be some surpassing effort, some risk. The hand moves, finds the lyre, and throws it upward with a fierce gesture. The lyre flies upward in night, whistling through the black air to become the constellation; as it goes up, hard, the four strings sing: *Eurydice.* And *then* the pieces begin to remember; they begin to come together; he turns into the god. He is music and poetry; he is Orpheus.

I was not able to write the poem. I went back to Chicago and to New York that winter, and, among a hundred crucial pressures, looked up some of the Orphic hymns in the New York Public Library. I wrote: "The mountaintop, in silence, after the murder" and "lions and towers of the sky" and "The pieces of the body begin to remember" and "He has died the death of the god." Now there begin to be notes. This is the middle of winter, six years after the night on Forty-Second Street.

Again in California, in a year of intense physical crisis, threat, renewal, loss, and beginning. Now the notes begin to be very full. He did not look at Eurydice. He looked past her, at Hell. Now the wounds are the chorus: Touch me! Love me! Speak to me! This goes back to the yearning and self-pity of early love poems, and a way must be found to end the self-pity.

Months later, the phrases begin to appear in fuller relationship. "The body as a circus, these freaks of Orpheus." Body Sonnets is one rejected notion. "Air-tree, nerve-tree, blood-maze"; Pindar said of him, "Father of Songs."

"Sing in me, days and voices," I write; and a form takes shape. I will solve a problem that has been moving toward solution. My longer poems, like the "Elegies" and "The Soul and Body of John Brown," contained songs. This poem will move toward its song: its own song and Orpheus' song. A poem that leads to a song! The pieces that come together, become a self, and sing.

Now I was ready to write. There were pages of notes and false starts, but there was no poem. There were whole lines, bits of drawing, telephone messages in the margin. Now something was ready; the poem began, and the first section was written.

It was slower to come to the second and third sections; as they were finished, the song too was ready; but now I turned into reader. The resurrection itself needed sharpening. These symbols must not be finished; the witness himself wants to finish. But this friend is right, the women must be part of his song, the god must include his murderers if murder is part of his life. And this correspondent is right, pain is not *forgotten*. All of this re-writing is conscious throughout, as distinct from the writing of the poem, in which suggestions, relations, images, phrases, sailed in from everywhere. For days of reminder and revery, everything became

Orpheus. Until it was time to go back to the title. The working
title was "Pieces of Orpheus." But that was for myself. No longer
the pieces, but the rebirth, stands clear. The name alone should
head the poem. So: two words are crossed out: it is ready.

THE POEM SEEN AS SYSTEM

The role of memory is not explored. We know the memory
of the unfinished act, or story, or joke, is stronger than that of the
finished. These symbols are never finished; they continue to
grow; perhaps that is their power. We know that the poetic strat-
egy, if one may call it that, consists in leading the memory of an
unknown witness, by means of rhythm and meaning and image
and coursing sound and always-unfinished symbol, until in a
blaze of discovery and love, the poem is taken. This is the music
of the images of relationship, its memory, and its information.

Functions of information and memory have been related in
Norbert Wiener's book of many sides and many excitements,
Cybernetics. Here, among a hundred suggestions, we hear the
"philosophical echoes" of "the transition from a Newtonian,
reversible time to a Gibbsian, irreversible time." We are shown
the necessity to be dynamically minded, and the line of one
philosopher is traced, from Leibniz' continuum of monads to the
post-Gibbsian dynamic interpretations. We meet again that hero
of our century, Clerk Maxwell's demon, and, confronted as he
is with his problems of entropy and equilibrium, we see something about the information which the sorting demon may
receive from particles approaching the gate he guards in his con-
tainer. We see that information here represents negative entropy.

Now a poem, like anything separable and existing in time,
may be considered as a system, and the changes taking place in
the system may be investigated. The notion of feedback, as it is
used in calculating machines and such linked structures as the

locks of the Panama Canal, is set forth. The relations of information and feedback in computing machines and the nervous system, as stated here, raise other problems. What are imaginative information and imaginative feedback in poetry? What are the emotional equivalents for these relationships? How far do these truths of control and communication apply to art?

The questions are raised, even with the older questions, like Proust's madeleine, still setting challenges to the sciences.

We know that the relationships in poetry are clearer when we think in terms of a dynamic system, whose tendencies toward equilibrium, and even toward entropy, are the same as other systems'. (Even Orpheus approached maximum entropy before he became a god.)

We know that poetry is not isolated here, any more than any phenomena can be isolated. Now again we see that all is unbegun.

The only danger is in not going far enough. The usable truth here deals with change. But we are speaking of the human spirit. If we go deep enough, we reach the common life, the shared experience of man, the world of possibility.

If we do not go deep, if we live and write half-way, there are obscurity, vulgarity, the slang of fashion, and several kinds of death.

All we can be sure of is that our art has life in time, it serves human meaning, it blazes on the night of the spirit; all we can be sure of is that at our most subjective we are universal; all we can be sure of is the profound flow of our living tides of meaning, the river meeting the sea in eternal relationship, in a dance of power, in a dance of love.

For this is the world of light and change: the real world; and the reality of the artist is the reality of the witnesses.

CHAPTER TWELVE

OUT OF CHILDHOOD

My one reader, you reading this book, who are you? what is your face like, your hands holding the pages, the child forsaken in you, who now looks through your eyes at mine?

Let me tell some of the childhood elements that have come into these pages, into this night with its intense side-long moon and the fast seafog flying over the city, this brilliant day with its unique light in the streets and parks, its light shed down to the Bay and to the red bridge, the hours sloping again to evening, when I knew I must write these words to you.

The curious thing is that whatever I wrote in early life has come true. Or is beginning to come true. The death of the lover, the son, the secret wound, the homesickness for New York, the reconciliation with everything evaded, even the poems that would lead to poems, and the moments of illumination followed by immeasurable setback, the Red Sea always followed by the Desert. And then there is the Promised Land. No, I do not believe in any Eden of the past. That garden is the future. Every year since my childhood has been better, in spite of the losses and mistakes. At least the questions have been clearer. As for the answers—But even they have come as questioning.

❂

The early days in the city. Stone, water, light. But also, the steep slope down to the river, the cattle cars bellowing in soft-colored morning. The water truck slanting a fountain, hard, on the black avenue. Sledding down snow on the slope. The sand quarries of my father, raw and yellow, far out of town, in the fields. The first public day, whose crowds filled the streets. They kissed each other and seemed to cry. I went out, yes I took a drum and it was a pleasure to beat it hard. Bong, bong. The old lady walked down the center of the traffic lane on Broadway; she was crying. My father and mother were out. Paper rained down.

That day was the False Armistice. The war was not yet over.

❂

You put your head back very far. There it was! The plane. With its double wings and a frail body. You could feel it in the back of your neck.

❂

The sands of summertime, the long ocean and sandbar. The Yacht Club, with its bait boxes at the end of the pier. Killies. Summer after summer, the pale hotels, yellow and white, the

boardwalks with the light striking down through the wet plank-
ing. Iodine smells, the breaker curling and down, seething away,
the little fish in the tide pools, and summer past summer, the
sandbar dissolving away. When the tide came in, you could still
run for the beach, ankle-deep in the deceptive foam.

⑥

The streets and the life of the child. Each of these apartment
houses, standing like dead trunks along the avenue, has its army
of children. Each gang, formed arbitrarily in one twelve-story
house, is set against all other gangs on the block and on the next
block. You fight the neighbor gang, on the brownstone stoops
between apartment houses; in winter, with snowballs. Ice may
be centered in the snowball. On Halloween, particularly, the
toughies from two avenues away. You must run; they have stock-
ings filled with flour; they will club you down.

⑥

You are a part of the city. New York is a part of you. For your
father is in the building business, and the skyscrapers are going
up. Your father can climb these skeletons, he laughs with the men
who are the bravest, the men who throw red-hot rivets with an
easy hook of the tongs, and the men who catch the rivets in a
bucket. In a tin can. High over the avenues, over the two rivers.

⑥

First reading, first music. The Victrola, the upright piano. A
book about a rabbit. The headlines: ALLIES ADVANCE
SIX MILES SOUTH TO SOISSONS.

❻

The school at the corner, chosen so that you need not cross the street and be in danger. The fire drill. We go down the stairs with our geography book, the drill waits until the book is balanced once more on the head.

Preparation for life.

❻

The maids and nurses and chauffeurs, those who most talk to you, who give you books to read. B., who comes from the Pyrenees, where they play jacks with knucklebones. H. and her mother, peaceable, Hungarian. The man who drives for us is Evelyn Nesbit's brother; you hear the details of the murder. Harry K. Thaw. The Woolworth Building.

❻

When your sister is born, you are seven. All your Oz books have disappeared to make room for the baby. They were the most important: those countries of magic, those immense living dolls, the adventure and decency, the implacable witches, and the endless traveling dreams.

❻

The city rises in its light. Skeletons of buildings; the orange-peel cranes; highways put through; the race of skyscrapers. And you are a part of this.

⊙

Before your birth, your parents knew the smaller cities. Father from Milwaukee, a Wisconsin whose cities were founded in 1848, the year his grandfather arrived; the violent legendary winters, ice-boats on the Lake, the newspaper route and all those hot fresh rolls. And the hard boyhood and difficult young manhood, turning into a salesman, alone, attached to his family, in New York, forming a partnership with Generoso Pope, and going on to identify with the building—the contracting for the building—of New York. And behind that, Bohemia, the river, the towns near Prague, the interview with Metternich of some unknown grandfather, who then must leave, overnight, for America.

Behind my mother, the simple Yonkers childhood, the years of clerical work, the ancestors. A silver goblet, hearsay of a cantor's songs, is all you know; then a gap of two thousand years until the Ancestor, Akiba, who fought to include the Song of Songs in the Bible, who was smuggled out of Jerusalem in a coffin by his disciples, who believed in Bar Cochba's revolution, who was tortured to death by his Roman friend, the general Rufus, until he said smiling: "The commandment says: Thou shalt love the Lord thy God with all thy heart, with all thy soul, and with all thy might. I have always loved Him with all my heart and with all my soul; now I know that I love Him with all my life." And he died.

⊙

The books. The translations Longfellow made. Poe's stories. Oscar Wilde's essays and fairy tales. All of Victor Hugo, and particularly *The Man Who Laughed*. Dickens, Dumas, the Book of Knowledge, and behind them all the Bible.

@

Knife and a fork.
A bottle and a cork.
And that's the way to
Spell New York—

@

Ibbety bibbety sibbety sab,
Ibbety bibbety kanaba,
Upsiderry,
Down the ferry,
Out goes Y—o—u.

@

Those are counting-out rhymes, and jump-rope rhymes. Their meaning is the rhythm of the game. (Years later, you see that "kanaba" was "canal boat," and "upsiderry" should have been "dictionary," or had been, but was no longer.) "Kaiser, Kaiser, turn around," is too close to your own name for comfort. There was some feeling against Germans in the recent war. Now, for your stamp collection, you acquire a new set of portrait stamps, all of men with flaring beards. Do their faces frighten you? You are told to be frightened. They are Bolsheviki. What are Bolsheviki?

@

One Saturday morning, you are late, and your father leaves for the office without taking you along. Usually, you walk with him for a few blocks, and then the car meets you, and you drive down to Fiftieth Street and the River, where The Office stands, with its garages filled with green and white trucks, and at the foot of the street, the great white or corn-yellow or gray mountains of sand and crushed rock.

This morning you are too late to catch up. You go on walking, determined not to be abandoned. You know you were not ready; and now you can not meet the car. The car has already somehow passed you; but you go on, ready to cry, unwilling to turn back. Suddenly the avenue changes, and you are half afraid, half caught up in excitement at a city where you had never walked. Here are the broken pavings of a wild, noisy, other world. Wide doors with welders' forges burning inside; the black caves of industrial garages; the autumn-colored trains bearing down the center of the street, clanging in red and brown and black, firing clouds up and behind; the barley-smelling tenements, shackled with fire escapes; the hard children running past you; and the harshness and clarity of this new city, the bitter marvelous struggle of a dream.

Now here is The Office, and you a different child.

6

The heroes are the Yankee baseball team, the Republican party, and the men who build New York City.

6

And Joan of Arc. In Domremy, as a little girl, she began to know what she had to do. Now you go to another school, a fine school, full of pictures on the walls, maps unrolled over the blackboard, many possible friends.

൬

Silence in the courtroom!
The judge wants to spit.

൬

Fire on the mountain.
Fire on the sea.
You can't catch me.

൬

Potsie is a hopscotch game played with a bit of slate. On certain days in the city, a wind turns back from Downtown, the sea flows over these parks and buildings, you know again you live in a harbor, you know your place is where a river meets the sea and a city is built.

Your nurses have their ways. They vanish quickly, as you begin to love them. One sits all day long on Riverside Drive while you play. Her head is back, her mouth is open. She is letting the sun shine down her throat. She used to be a singer, and she wants her lost voice to come back.

One punishes you because you have called her name out loud in the street. That brings bad luck.

One accuses your father of hypnotizing your mother's friend to death. She leaves quickly; she is in love with her doctor, who has been "giving her pills."

൬

You were born in the house where Gyp the Blood lived. The

people you know in this house are the janitor's son, who helps you raise your one-eyed chick; Ted Lewis, the bandleader; the neighbors' children, who are very heroic in the house gang. From cellar to cellar of the enormous buildings, interminable war; one day you are locked into the cellars of a strange house, and must work your way through the tunnels, past the intense furnaces, to the court and over the iron gates to the open street.

⊙

Nobody suspects that there are living artists and living poets. All are dead: the musicians, the poets, the sculptors. This is a world of business. Reality is the city; real men go to The Office.

Poetry does not enter the life of anyone you see, except as spoken bits of Owen Meredith, Bryant, Robert Service, Elizabeth Barrett Browning. Except in the servants' rooms: what do you hear there? *The Man With the Hoe, The Ballad of Reading Gaol.* The little five-cent books, smelling of castor oil, are read and re-read. In the families you know, the sets of books in the front, bought as furniture—the piano is furniture of the same order—are rarely opened. No reading, in these houses, or in yours, until, at a stroke, your mother begins to read Emerson and the Bible, to revive a lost interest in her religion, and slowly to move, without direction, and years later, after the family breaks, to move forward in her development, as so many of these women move, at their first chance, in their fifties or their sixties.

⊙

Building is booming. The highways reach out, skyscrapers begin in these deep-cut foundations, down to Manhattan bed-rock and beyond, bridges are planned. Concrete must contain expansion joints, the strips of material that allow the forcing heat of these summers, the forcing cold of these violent white winters, to do their work. The principle of the expansion joint, you learn, runs through all.

There is a terrible moment in *The Blue Bird* when the graves are about to open.

The river, and the city, and the sea. They are always beautiful, in their many lights and in their darknesses.

⑥

But there are living poets!

And now the poems that you have been making, ever since the beginning, have their sense, they can be shown. Now I can say "I," although in the unguarded moments, in the questioning, the "you" is the one asked. I show the best poems of my tenth year, in a little notebook, to my teacher. There is a picture of a Buddha under the glass of her desk; she calls us to quiet by ringing a gong shaped like a dark bowl; when I come to school with red eyes she speaks to me very kindly.

She has a scuffle with D., the bad boy of the class; she cuffs him—she who is always contained, and gentle!—and leads him out, howling. She comes back. "Write what you saw," she said. We do write; and no two accounts agree. "That was staged," she says after we read our reports. "Now we will begin our study of the American Revolution. These are the sources we will use…"

⑥

We are asked about a clock which many of us pass on the way to school. We are asked to vote: are the figures on the clock Roman numerals or Arabic numerals. All those who take that road to school vote: we are almost evenly divided. "Now look at the clock, on your way home." I walk up Broadway. The clock's dial is legible: its hands tell the time by pointing to the letters HOTEL ALAMAC.

A teacher asks: "How many of you know any other road in the city except the road between home and school?" I do not put up my hand.

These are moments at which one begins to see.

⊚

I have always been well, and always been strong. The maids and chauffeurs who were my friends told me their stories before they married or committed suicide. All the time, I was writing poems. There were the red-headed boy C., the black-haired boy J., the beautiful girl J.; all these I loved wordlessly from afar.

⊚

Now there are cars, and country clubs: the long trimmed fields edged with tall grass, sand traps, interrupted by little lakes.

The two sacred things, taboo, never to be discussed, are money and sex. A young girl is supposed to know these facts about the people she meets: what sex they are, whether they have money, how old they are. Everybody else knows facts, popular songs, jokes.

An aunt defends me to my parents. There is constant need of defense. We seem physically close, in our family, although nobody is supposed to be "demonstrative"; it is conversation that is lacking. For a long time I imagine the farthest intimacy in terms of perfectly open talk at the dinner table.

But the days of crowding in the baby's room with the nurse,

and going to school in the Pierce, are over. There is a different apartment, high over the river. The far plains and domes of New Jersey, the train barges on the river, the moving lights of the river signs, are all clear as glass in this air.

There is deep estrangement in all the houses I know. Money is seen as the estranger.

Now the skyscrapers go up, my cousin sells out to Hearst, Valentino is dead and the women push over the cars in a blast of grief; Sacco and Vanzetti are dead, and something is signified by this that cannot be put aside; Caruso is long dead, but we remember, and Gatti-Casazza gives us his book of caricatures. The B.P.M. plate goes up on the car, and we are privileged to drive through lights.

The winter afternoons, waiting in front of the car entrance to Altman's, with the pale ivory-cool tab in one's hand, as the numbers flash on the board of lights. Going to the Museum, along the row of cat-headed deities, to the Gianpietrino Madonna, to the "Descent Into Hell," to the Contemporary Design show, and the Spanish show. Listening to sermons every week, or reading the Bible during these sermons, among a congregation whose watered-down faith leaves hardly anything besides business custom, and camouflage, except during one month of turning and renewal.

There are Shelley and Keats, every word of their poems.

There are Mantegna and Pollaiuolo.

There is the Park with its groves and lakes, its little capes of stone.

There are the cement mixers, turning and turning as they ride through the streets, and the broad metal strips which read: SERVICE. And the murdering years of this business, the competitors outdone, the leap up with the Walker rule, the questions that Carlo Tresca later asked me, which never were answered.

And a few friends, their homes in the afternoons, the music. The Ravel "Pavane," the "Jeune Fille aux Cheveux de Lin." And, at home, governesses, violin practice of H., while I read Chesterton and Chaucer and *Of Human Bondage*, and *The Romance of Leonardo da Vinci*.

⑥

The dead vagrant, killed by hunger, found starved to death outside the full locked warehouse.

⑥

Subway, the hurling of lights in the curved blackness, the passengers' acquiescence, the beating yellow dimness in the trains. An open wound outside the school building, where they dug and blasted for a new line. Stones shattering the braced window of a classroom. No, this is not a wound: this is an origin.

⑥

The building of the Bridge, past which we drove to the new school at Fieldston every day. The towers, which were never covered, which rose in their driven naked beauty, and the hundreds of hooks inverted in the concrete piles. Finally, cables, a slender roadbed, the long arc across the Hudson.

A moment at which I knew there would always be poetry. The quarrel with M.; how she threatened never to speak to me again except on one condition: that I promise not to write these poems. I do not remember the quarrel; I remember that she wrote far better than I, and that the threat to be cut off seemed a real threat. I promised. For four weeks, I was not troubled. A promise given becomes so binding that there is no difficulty in keeping it. But, at the end of that time, a poem began, and the trouble with it. For two weeks, I wrestled with my word, with the poem, with all the risks, and I did not know who I was. At the end of six weeks, there was no longer any choice. I got up in the night, and wrote the poem down. The next day I told M. that I could no longer keep the promise. "What promise?" she asked.

⊙

I think there is choice possible at any moment to us, as long as we live. But there is no sacrifice. There is a choice, and the rest falls away. Second choice does not exist. Beware of those who talk about sacrifice.

⊙

And first death seen. The great winds blowing along the River, singing in the windows on the Drive, holding their high notes through the keyholes, with all the rooms of our protected houses exposed to death and the wind.

⊙

The books being Blake, D. H. Lawrence, Proust.
The flaming torch of the Sherry Netherlands Tower.
The race between the Chrysler and Empire State Buildings.
Movies: *Metropolis*, *The Crowd*.
The symphony as a regular function, first a river of sensation, then the boredom of a habit, and then, with an adaptive gesture, a coming into focus, a sudden opening to music.
And the bookshop of Mr. O'Malley, a cool, cavernous,

traditional secondhand bookstore on Amsterdam Avenue near Seventy-Fifth Street, where I began to spend many afternoons, for the O'Malley family adopted me, and let me listen, and read, and soon help a little.

⊚

Contemporary poetry is reached, in the fresh anthologies by Untermeyer and Aiken, in the Modern Library, and then in all the books at school and here. MacLeish's *Hamlet* is new, and Jeffers' *Tamar* and *Roan Stallion* and *The Tower Beyond Tragedy.* McKnight Black is publishing, and D. H. Lawrence, and we read *Prufrock* together.

⊚

To have loved the caddy at the country club, Russell, and listened to his stories as we lounged in the high sea-grass. And, filled with love and worship and helplessness, to have pitied him as his father drank his earnings down. And made plans as we told our fortunes in the clouds, or swam in the weedy Bay, or walked over the docks of oyster shells. And have left him at the end of summer.

⊚

As I tell about it now, they alternate, the sense of excitement and the sense of discomfort, in memory. The bare branches and the poems; the man in the little railroad hut and his love affair with a schoolteacher up the river; the two whores on our block, Black Chiffon and Yellow Hat; the grocery stores where the respectable unconscious women and the kept women and the madams marketed together; the drugstore where we drank our sodas, which I later, at the Luciano trial, learned was the all-night center—during all those years—of the narcotics and prostitution industries of New York; the clumsiness, in the face of their families' hopes for a quiet, eligible, bridge-playing future, of the gifted girls and boys. There was a sense of discomfort in some of us, sunk deep in the nap of the "comfortable life"; all we knew was that we were not comfortable.

All I knew was that. The first gestures were the clumsy, groping ones of protest, in my first poems as at my first dance.

There were the marvelous chances: the hours near the river in the country, when my school moved just outside the city. The discovery, late, of school libraries and public libraries. The first hearing of *Sacre du Printemps*. The excellent physics lab, and Frank Oppenheimer working at the next table, and the explosive splash on the ceiling of which we used to say: "See that? That's Frank." Janice Loeb, bursting with all the concerns which would lead her to film, talking Jeffers and Despiau, Renoir, Matisse, Stravinsky; she took her temperature before and after reading certain poems; she could send it up one degree, Fahrenheit; that impressed us inordinately.

when the world rode in, as in the poems rode

And Elinor Goldmark, teaching English; and Henry Simon, teaching English and Sonata Form. And Dudley Fitts, coming to school to take apart "Trees":…it is nursing, its arms are up, it is looking at God, it is living-with rain, this nursing creature has snow on its bosom…. Do you see it? And John Lovejoy Elliott and Felix Adler showing us Father Damien, and Pasteur, and Stevenson, and *The Dream of John Ball*, and *The Harbor*. And the productions of *Midsummer Night's Dream* and *Everyman*. There were the moments of perception.

⑥

Then after one summer at a camp in Maine, I visited the family of the F. sisters, and for the first time saw a household in which all the members shared these excitements. We went to the theater and Mr. F. spoke of his latest case, a labor case he was to win well; and Mrs. F. as we drove that night to Westchester, let down her hair in the car; it streamed back, near my face, colored in the night. I had never seen anyone's mother do that. The next day, they showed me the book of D. H. Lawrence's paintings for the first time. We went back to the city, and I learned that people lived below Fifty-Seventh Street, below Fourteenth Street. I learned that I had been brought up as a protected, blindfolded daughter, who might have finally learned some road other than that between school and home, but who knew nothing of people, of New York, or of herself. Everything was to be begun; not only that, but unlearned, and then at last begun.

⑥

To come to college was to enter the world of people. Locked in, with the keyword *protection,* asking too much of friends. I had kept myself away. The first day at college ended childhood.

Then I began to write the poems that are in my first book.

⑥

The images of personal love and freedom, controlled as water is controlled, as the flight of planes is controlled. The images of relationship, in which the ancestor carried out of Jerusalem and the unborn son may meet; the music of the images of relationship.

Experience taken into the body, breathed in, so that reality is the completion of experience, and poetry is what is produced. And life is what is produced.

To stand against the idea of the fallen world, a powerful and destructive idea overshadowing Western poetry. In that sense, there is no lost Eden, and God is the future. The child walled-up in our life can be given his growth. In this growth is our security.

"A poet has to undergo a process of birth and growth: he does not discover himself until he has rejected the alternate selves represented by the poetry already existing in the world," says Herbert Read. These selves are represented by all the idols ringing our childhood: we can make autobiographies of a parade of symbols. The drum, the sidewalk, the river, the tower, the father, the car, the aunt, the chauffeur, the sister, the mother, the book, the piano, the harbor, the slum, the sand hill, the lake, the cement mixer, the sacred dome, the school door, the museum stair, the field of coarse grass, the golf green, the Bridge, the poem written in the dark, the unsolved murder, the corner whore, stain on the lab ceiling, the granite mountain under whose cliff the adolescent all night lay, waiting to climb in the morning light.

Have I spoken of Baldface? of Emerald Pool?

Of the climb up Mount Washington?

How can I look back and not speak of the stupid learning about birth? Of the stupid learning that people make love, and how it seemed the reason for all things, the intimacy of my wondering, the illumination that—to an adolescent—was the cause for life around me, the reason why the unhappy people I knew did not kill themselves?

Looking back from what I knew in Spain, I must remember the silent storms of puberty, the unleashed marvel of power that could only wreck what I knew, a world of constriction and fear, a materialist world that exposed the American danger, in materialism, to be mystical about material values.

The real-estate crash and the stock-market crash ripped open the veils of that world.

Our drive was not for the old unity. We had entered the age of the long war and the circular traps: unemployment which branded these children with a sense of waste that dragged back each drop of blood; silence among all the shouting and the floods of print that renewed a distrust of all beliefs and all poetry; and beyond all of this, a sense of human possibility that would not let us rest in defeat ever, or admit the notion of defeat. In art, of course, the mysticism of success and failure will not hold. The world of business is open warfare, cold iron through every throat, and the battle shriek "Success!" But in art, these terms cannot apply. One works on oneself; one writes the poem, makes the movie, paints; and one is changed in the process.

The work is what we wanted, and the process. We did not want a sense of Oneness with the One so much as a sense of Many-ness with the Many. Multiplicity no longer stood *against* unity. Einstein, Picasso, Joyce, gave us our keys; the nature of motion reached us from Proust as from the second-run movie; the Hippodrome girls went down into the eternal lake, Lindbergh had conquered time, Roosevelt had at last spoken openly to us of the demon of our house, and he had named it: fear.

Against this would always stand the sense of wonder and range in New York, of both my parents, and of my childhood. The world could find an image, infinite as the flower, in this city; the city could find an image, eternal as change, in this meeting-place of sea and river, with their magnificence and filth among the growing.

But our youth and our time had shown us that images were only one beginning. The century had shown us that there were many ways of selling out, many careers for the corrupted consciousness.

Those of us whose imaginations had been reached would not sell out: we would not stop at the images, or at "sincerity," at security, or at any one field. There are relationships, we said, to be explored; and in our weakness and limitation, in ignorance and several poverties and doubt and disgust, we thought of possibility.

CHAPTER THIRTEEN

MEANINGS OF PEACE

The identified spirit, man and woman identified, moves toward further identifications. In a time of long war, surrounded by the images of war, we imagine peace. Among the resistances, we imagine poetry. And what city makes the welcome, in what soil do these roots flourish?

For our concern is with sources.

The sources of poetry are in the spirit seeking completeness. If we look for the definitions of peace, we will find, in history, that they are very few. The treaties never define the peace they bargain for: their premise is only the lack of war. The languages sometimes offer a choice of words: in the choice is illumination. In one long-standing language there are two meanings for peace. These two provide a present alternative. One meaning of peace is offered as "rest, security." This is comparable to our "security, adjustment, peace of mind." The other definition of peace is this: peace is completeness.

It seems to me that this belief in peace as completeness belongs to the same universe as the hope for the individual as full-valued.

In what condition does poetry live? In all conditions, sometimes with honor, sometimes underground. That history is in our poems.

THE CLIMATE OF POETRY

In what climate, poetry? Some will say, the climate of slavery, where the many feed the few, and the few explore their arts and their sciences. Fashionable now again, the talk of the elite reaches politics and education.

Some will say, in the wide-open boom times of a patron system: the historic heights of a building Church, the Renaissance of the small acquisitive states, the times when the bankers founded their galleries, and the prize of nations is their art.

Some will say, in the pit of suffering, when all is lost but the central human fire, when the deliverers come, speaking in the holy symbols of risk and life and everything made sacred.

But we know the partial truth in each of these. We know the slaveholder minds among us, contriving their elite, copying and multiplying natural waste, and believing that meaning can always be put off. These people insist, "He is so great a poet, you need not hear what he says." They are, in their contempt for value, armed. They have whips in their hands. I shall not say they are enemies of poetry; although they are. Only see the effect of their poets on these men: the literature of aversion, guilt, and the longing for forgiveness does its work on the writers and on the witnesses. Its work is tragic; contempt is bred here, and remorse, the dead scatterings. At its best, the poems are those of power and love.

We know the men who need the times of profit; the moment these years fade, they tell us there is no place now for humor, there is no place for poetry. They try to make humor and rage and poetry luxury products. But this cannot be done. At its best, the poems are those of vitality and love.

We know, too, those who are warped until suffering is what they need. We have seen an "occasional verse" grow up of depression and of war. One of the worst things that could happen to our poetry at this time would be for it to become an occasional poetry of war. A good deal of the repugnance to the social poetry of the 1930's was caused by reactionary beliefs; but as much was caused, I think, because there were so many degrees of blood-savagery in it, ranging all the way from self-pity—naked or identified with one victim after another—to actual blood-lust and display of wounds, a rotten sort of begging for attention and sympathy in the name of an art that was supposed to produce action. This was not confined to "social" literature; you may see the style of self-pity in many of the "realistic" novels and confessions of these years. But, fundamentally, this literature is purified to compassion. At its best, the poems are those of offering and love.

We need a background that will let us find ourselves and our poems, let us move in discovery. The tension between the parts of such a society is health; the tension here between the individual and the whole society is health. This state arrives when freedom is a moving goal, when we go beyond the forms to an organic structure which we can in conscience claim and use. Then the multiplicities sing, each in his own voice. Then we understand that there is not meaning, but meanings; not liberty, but liberties. And multiplicity is available to all. Possibility joins the categorical imperative. Suffering and joy are fused in growth; and growth is the universal.

A society in motion, with many overlapping groups, in their dance. And above all, a society in which peace is not lack of war, but a drive toward unity.

WAR AND WEAKNESS

Always our wars have been our confessions of weakness. They have not been like the individual's need for action; they have been like our traditional need for confession to another person, but carried further and made grotesque. They have been like the cascades of guilt and self-punishment that certain psychotic criminals have been known to pour out before their judgment.

Those psychiatrists who have been working for more than adjustment in the individual have understood the role of confession. And we all have been aware that action, taken in time, is the child of appropriate response: we then stop fascism as it begins, taproot by taproot in our daily lives, and never need to go to war with each other, pouring out in death our bombs, our plagues, the men and women of our future.

The appropriate release of our decisive forces, and the confession carried to its most human chance. Do these have anything to do with war and peace? Do they have anything to do with poetry?

CONFESSION AND TESTIMONY

Confession to another person, to a priest or a psychiatrist, is full of revelation. The self-understanding that comes with the form, with the relation made among memory, conscience, and imagination, brings cure and forgiveness! These are the places where "sooth" and "soothe" meet; places of truth and healing. Confession to divinity, to the essential life of what one loves and hopes, on a level other than the human, is full of revelation. The detachment, here, from conscious and unconscious emotional values, has power to change one's life.

But there is another confession, which is the confession to oneself made available to all. This is confession as a means to understanding, as testimony to the truths of experience as they become form and ourselves. The type of this is the poem; in which the poet, intellectually giving form to emotional and imaginative experience, with the music and history of a lifetime behind the work, offers a total response. And the witness receives the work, and offers a total response, in a most human communication.

AN APPROPRIATE AGGRESSION

Such action does release aggression; or, rather, the making of a poem is the type of action which releases aggression. Since it is released appropriately, it is creation.

For the last time here, I wish to say that we will not be saved by poetry. But poetry is the type of the creation in which we may live and which will save us.

THINGS NEAR THEIR BIRTH

The world of this creation, and its poetry, is not yet born.

The possibility before us is that now we enter upon another time, again to choose. Its birth is tragic, but the process is ahead: we must be able to turn a time of war into a time of building.

There are the wounds: they are crying everywhere. There are the false barriers: but they are false. If we believe in the unity and multiplicity of the world, if we believe in the unity and multiplicity of man, then we believe too in the unity and multiplicity of imagination. And we will speak across the barriers, many to many. The great ideas are always emerging, to be available to all men and women. And one hope of our lives is the communication of these truths.

THE LIFE OF POETRY

To be against war is not enough, it is hardly a beginning. And all things strive; we who try to speak know the ideas trying to be more human, we know things near their birth that try to become real. The truth here goes farther, there is another way of being against war and for poetry.

We are against war and the sources of war.

We are for poetry and the sources of poetry.

They are everyday, these sources, as the sources of peace are everyday, infinite and commonplace as a look, as each new sun.

POETRY AND PEACE

As we live our truths, we will communicate across all barriers, speaking for the sources of peace. Peace that is not lack of war, but fierce and positive.

We hear the saints saying: Our brother the world. We hear the revolutionary: Dare we win?

All the poems of our lives are not yet made.

We hear them crying to us, the wounds, the young and the unborn—we will define that peace, we will live to fight its birth, to build these meanings, to sing these songs.

Until the peace makes its people, its forests, and its living cities; in that burning central life, and wherever we live, there is the place for poetry.

And then we will create another peace.

San Francisco
July 1949

ACKNOWLEDGMENTS
1949

I wish to make acknowledgment to the following authors and publishers for selections quoted in this book from:

Indians of the Americas, Copyright, 1947 by John Collier; published by the New American Library of World Literature and W. W. Norton and Company; *The Principles of Art* by R. G. Collingwood, used by permission of the Clarendon Press, Oxford; *American Renaissance* by F. O. Matthiessen, Copyright 1941 by Oxford University Press, Inc.; *Our Inner Conflicts* by Karen Horney, used by permission of W. W. Norton and Company; *Leaves of Grass* by Walt Whitman, used by permission of Doubleday & Company; *The Film Sense* by Sergei Eisenstein, used by permission of Harcourt, Brace and Company; *To All Hands* by John Mason Brown, published by Whittlesey House, Copyright, 1943; *Music of Young Children* by G. E. Moorhead and Donald Pond, used by permission of The Pillsbury Foundation; *The Migration of Symbols* by Donald Mackenzie, used by permission of Routledge & Kegan Paul Ltd.; *The Innocent Eye* by Herbert Read, published by The Macmillan Company; *Collected Poems* by Hart Crane, published by the Liveright Company; *On Growth and Form* by D'Arcy Wentworth Thompson, The Macmillan Company; *The Poetic Image* by C. Day Lewis, Oxford University Press; *The Social Neurosis* by Trigant Burrow, used by permission of the author; *The Constitution* by Woodrow Wilson; *Letters of Herman Melville* and *Battle-Pieces* and *Aspects of War,* Harper & Brothers; Navajo Creation Myth by Hastiin Klah, translated by Harry Hoijer, recorded by Mary C. Wheelright, the Museum of Navajo Ceremonial Arts; *American Building* by James Marston Fitch, Houghton Mifflin Company; *Bolts of Melody* by Emily Dickinson, used by permission of Harper & Brothers; *Summertime* by Ira Gershwin, Copyright 1935 by Gershwin Publishing Corporation, New York, N.Y., used by permission; *Essays, Ancient and Modern* by T. S. Eliot, Harcourt, Brace and Company; *You're the Top* by Cole Porter; *Negro Folk Songs as Sung by Leadbelly,* edited by John A. Lomax and Alan Lomax, The Macmillan Company; *The Blues* by Abbe Niles, Albert and Charles Boni; *People and Power* by Harvey Fergusson, William Morrow; *Mourning Becomes Electra* and *The Iceman Cometh* by Eugene O'Neill, Random House; *Another Part of the Forest* and *Watch on the Rhine* by Lillian Hellman, Random House; *The Skin of Our Teeth* by Thornton Wilder, Harper & Brothers; *All My Sons* by Arthur Miller, Harcourt, Brace and Company; *Mother, What Is Man?* by Stevie Smith, Chatto & Windus; *Documentary Film* by Paul Rotha, W. W. Norton and Company; *Logic of the Sciences and the Humanities* by F. S. C. Northrop, The Macmillan Company; *The Chinese Written Character as a Medium for Poetry* by Ernest Fenollosa, Stanley Nott; *Collected Papers* by Charles Peirce, Harvard University Press; *Cybernetics* by Norbert Wiener, The Technology Press and John Wiley; *An Essay on Literature by Pu Chu'i* by Shih Hsiang Chen, used by permission of the author.

1996

⟲

Excerpts from this edition of *The Life of Poetry* have appeared in *The American Poetry Review*, *The American Voice*, and *Poetry Flash*.

⟲

Paris Press gratefully acknowledges the generous assistance of William L. Rukeyser. We also offer our deepest thanks to the individuals who helped in the production of this book, most especially Rebecca Bell, Kim Albertson, Amy Ware, Anne Goldstein, Myra Shapiro, and Sawnie Morris.

INDEX

surroundings, 148; vs. tyranny, 93
Freud, Sigmund, 12
Frost, Robert, 53

Galton, Francis, 134
García Lorca, Federico, 87, 108, 110, 130
Germany, Nazi, 36
Gershwin, George and Ira, 108
Gibbs, Willard, xix, xxii, xxiv, 11, 164,
167; Rukeyser's biography of, xiii,
xxviii, 95-96
Gluck, Christoph Williband von, 182
Good: concept of, 64; vs. evil, xxiii;
problem of, in Whitman, xxiii, 72-75
Graham, Martha, 130
Grapes of Wrath, The, xxii
Graphics Workshop, 136, 137
Graves, Morris, 136
Greenough, Horatio, 88, 89
Guilt, accusations of by critics, 47, 48

Handy, W. C., 109, 110
Hariot, Thomas, xix
Hartley, Marsden, 135
Hawthorne, Nathaniel, xix, 27
Hays code, 45
Hellman, Lillian, 124, 128
Helmholtz, Hermann von, 115
Heroes, as images, 35-37
Hiroshima, 160
History, songs from, 85-86
Hitchcock, Alfred, 143, 144
Hitler, Adolf, 42
Hoijer, Harry, 87
Hollywood, 45, 46, 141; writer in, 146-
147. See also Movies
Hopkins, Gerard Manley, 32, 78, 171
Hopscotch, 196
Horney, Karen, 12, 44
Houdini, Harry, xix
Hughes, Langston, 110, 138
Human being: and reality of relation-
ships, 165; full-valued, 49, 56, 209
Humanity: common life of, 187; primi-
tive, 41-42, 177; tendency of art and
religion toward, 40-41; unity of, 162

Iceman Cometh, The (E. O'Neill), 124
Idiot's Delight (R. Sherwood), 126-127
Illness, and breakdown of communication, 54
Image(s), 32-35, 207; flow of, and language,
137-138, 153; historical lives as, 35-37;
history of, 23-24; our lives as, 40; and

message, 168; motion of, 169-171; in
movies, 141-148; in pictures, 133-141,
170; in poetry, 39-40, 83,133, 178-180,
169, 170, 181
Imagination, 7; American, xix; falsehood impossible in, 49; in full-valued
human being, 56; impoverished, 21, 43-
44, 50, 52, 160; in painting, 29; and
poetry, 80, 133; as reality of arts, 30; as
scientific faculty, 163-165; and selling
out, 208; senses used in, 80; unity of,
162-163; value of, 29, 56, 208
Immortality, of poems, 62
Indians (American). See Tribes, North
American indigenous
"In Hades, Orpheus" (Rukeyser), 182
Ives, Charles, xix, 97

James, William, 161
Javitz, Romana, 138
Jazz, xx; linkage of words and music in,
113
Jeffers, Robinson, 83, 127, 164, 203, 204
Jefferson, Blind Lemon, 111
Jews, 9, 36
Joan of Arc, xviii, 195
Jokes, and aversion to emotion, 45
Jones, Robert Edmond, 129
Juggling, rhythm of, 130

Kauffer, E. McKnight, 138
Kaye, Danny, 130
Kelly, Gene, xx
Klah, Hastiin, 87
Knowledge, division of, 13; poetry as, 7
Kramrisch, 154, 155

Language: broken, 123-124; as carrier
for emotion, 126; and flow of images,
153; as fossil poetry, 166-167; with Jewish
inflection, 126; lack of reliance on, 123,
127; life in, 172; as meaning, 127; and
mental illness, 54-55; in movies, 153;
symbols in, 166; in theater, 122-127; of
transformation, xxii. See also Word(s)
Lawrence, D. H., 171, 202, 205
Leadbelly, xx, 111
Leibniz, Gottfried Wilhelm, 186
Lewis, Cecil Day, 39, 91
Lies, 42, 48; protection against, 45-47.
See also Falsehood
Life Is Beautiful, 144
Lincoln, Abraham, 35, 36, 78
Lives, creation of in poetry, 172

experiences evoked by, 134-135; images in, 170; representational, 154; as visual art, 29; and writing, 134, 138, 170

Paisan, 145

Passion of Joan of Arc, The 145

Past, recovery of, xix

Pattern, of space on page, 117. See also Rhythm

Pauses, 117

Payne, Robert, 131

Peace: definition of, 209; as drive for unity, 211; as final word, xxvi; need for idea of, 30; poetry and, xvii, xxvi, 214

Percival, James Gates, 89, 92-94, 170

Perfection: aiming for, 16; and death as alternative, 53, 83

Photographs: xviii, 138-141; captions for, 141; sequences of, 139-140

Pierce, Charles, 174

Pirandello, 128, 151

Poe, Edgar Allan, xix, 67, 193

Poem(s): appropriate expression in, 169; arrangement of, 19, 167-168; availability of, 174; continuity in, 141; creation of, 142, 169, 172, 173, 178, 186, 205-206, 210; delayed appreciation of, 89-90; energy transfer in, 173; form of, 171; "idea" for, 181; ideas in, 33; images in, 83, 170; immortality of, 62; interdependences in, 169; lost, 91; material made of, 179-180; as meeting-places, xxvi; as object, 174; organic nature of, xxii,171; printed vs. spoken, 79-80; as process, 174; in public domain, 97; as release of aggression, xxvi, 213; rewriting of, 185; and song, 117-118; truth of, 32; and unconscious, 181; wall display of enlarged, 138

Poet(s): breathing rhythm of, 117; dead vs. living, 197, 198; growth of, 206; imagist, 133; as prophet, 92; as provider of meaning, 13, 132; relation with nature, 53; relation with poem and audience, 174, 175, 178; self-pitying, 176; truth of, 55-56

Poetry: abstract, 115; accusations about, 46, 47, 167; as art, 25, 168; attitude of, 8; audience of, 23, 54; and aversion to emotion, 45; in Bible, 83, 131; and belief, 39-40; blues as tradition of, 109-113; and charge of obscurity, xxi, 10, 11, 18, 54, 109; and children, xxi, 9-10; climate for, 3, 210-211; combining music and meaning, 32-33, 167-168, 172; concern of for meaning, 13, 20, 161, 169; and culture in conflict, 61-64; dance rhythms in,

88; difficulties in, 141; emotions in, 19, 21, 172; enemies of, 210; failure of, 23, 62; fear of, xx, xxi, 7-11, 14-17, 30, 44; in films, 153; form in, xxv, 20, 171; hunger for, 159; imagist, 133; juxtapositions in, 19; love vs. hatred of, 9; and memory, 116; in music, 105; and peace, 214; professed ignorance about, 16; on radio, 118, 131; reading of, 117; resemblance of to love, 20; resistance to, xxii, 8-11; as resource, 7; response to, 11; and science, 159-161, 176; social, 211; as sounds in motion, 171; sources of, 209-211; speaking for the wordless, 132; spoken vs. written, 29, 131; subject of, 53; theater of, 127; time for, 10; unity of, xxvii; use of, xxiv; and war, xx, 9, 53, 78-79, 210-211; as words, 166; workshop, 178-179. See also Meter; Rhythm; Song; Word(s)

Poincaré, Henri, 165, 169

Pond, Donald, 105, 107

Possibility: history of, 61; Whitman as poet of, xxiii

"Prometheus" (J. G. Percival), 92-94

Proust, Marcel, 24, 187, 202

Psychoanalysis, 24, 55

Punctuation: as biological, 117; silence and, 116

Radio, 17, 45, 105; poetry on, 118, 131

Raleigh, Sir Walter, 33

Read, Herbert, 9, 206

Reader: address to, 189; and difficulties in poem, 141; elite, 146; and moment of poem's impact, 31-32; poem in imagination of, 178; and punctuation, 117; rights of, 95, 97. See also Audience

Reality: and art, 154, 155; and experience, 177; and fear of poetry, 30

Relations/relationships: in art, 12; images of, 205; need to explore, 208; pleasure in, 145; poem as system of, xxvii; science as system of, xxv, 165-167; survival value of, 177

Religion(s): former utility of, 163; ideas of available to all, 8; images of, 83

Republican party, 195

Response, poetry's demand for, xxv, 11

Rhyme(s), 33, 171, 176; children's, 10, 91, 106, 194

Rhythm(s), xxv, 32-33, 88, 115, 175, 176, 186; bodily, 77-78, 116; children's sense of, 107; in children's songs, 105; of

121, 122; musical comedy, 129-130; poetry of, 127; weakness of, 121
"Theory of Flight" (Rukeyser), xvii
Theory of Flight (Rukeyser), xxi-xxii
Thirty-Nine Steps, The, 143
Thompson, D'Arcy Wentworth, xxv, 38, 171
Thoreau, Henry David, xix
Thought: art as preparation for, 25, 26; shared, 46, 53. See also Consciousness
Time: arrangements of, 31; image in, 33; Newtonian vs. Gibbsian, 186; for poetry, 10
Tribes, North American indigenous, xix; chants of, xx, 86-88, 130; creation myths of, 86; dream-singing, 91-92; Navajo, 87; relationship of to our society, 44
Truth: as agreement of components, 167; and communication, 27; death as, 83; in different times, 31; of experience, 8, 212; imaginative, 32, 55-56; and message of poem, 168-169; search for, 146; usable, 8, 26-27

Un-American Activities Committee, 17
United States: government of, and Newtonian theory, 63; and mysticism about material values; 206; poetry in life of, 8
Unity: drive toward, 211; of humanity, 162; of imagination, 162-163; and multiplicity, 207, 213; of nature, 162; of poetry, xxvii; of science, xxvii, 162; principle of, 63; in Whitman, 78
Untermeyer, Louis, 91

War: and concern with meaning, 20; idea of, xxii, 61; and ideas to be fought for, 137; and imagination, 30; memory of, 1-2; vs. peace, 209, 211, 214; perpetual, 61; plays dealing with meaning of, 127; and poetry, xvi, 9, 53, 69, 78-79, 210-211; Rukeyser and, xiv, vii; and thirst for poetry, xvi; turned into time of building, 213; as weakness, 211; in Whitman, 78-79
Watch on the Rhine (L. Hellman), 124-125
Weather, 13
Welles, Orson, 129, 152
Whitman, Walt, xix, xxv, 26, 62, 66, 75-83, 88, 89, 138; acceptance of self in, xxiii, 77; as poet of possibility, x, xxiii, 82-84; and problem of good,

xxiii, 72-75
Wiener, Norbert, 186
Wilder, Thornton, 125
Williams, Tennessee, 128
Willkie, Wendell, xix
Wilson, E. B., 95
Wilson, Woodrow, 63-64, 163
"Windhover, The" (G. M. Hopkins), 32
Witness, to poetry, 174-175. See also, Audience
Woman Alone, A, 143-144
Word(s): and abstract poetry, 115; combined with music, 113, 132, 167; poetry as, 13, 132, 166; in songs, 113; search for, 116. See also Language
World War II, xviii, 9
Writing: of advertising, 140, 147; and arts of sight, 133; as aspect of giving, 55; in Hollywood, 146-147; and movie sound tracks, 152; and pictures, 134, 137-139; re-writing, 51
Wyatt, Sir Thomas, 34

Yankees, New York, 195
Yeats, W. B., 128, 131, 171